The Secret Meaning of Money

Cloé Madanes
with Claudio Madanes

The Secret
Meaning
of Money

 Jossey-Bass Publishers
San Francisco

Substantial discounts on bulk quantities of Jossey-Bass books are available to corporations, professional associations, and other organizations. For details and discount information, contact the special sales department at Jossey-Bass Inc., Publishers. (415) 433–1740; Fax (415) 433–0499.

For sales outside the United States, contact your local Paramount Publishing International office.

Manufactured in the United States of America. Nearly all Jossey-Bass books and jackets are printed on recycled paper containing at least 10 percent postconsumer waste, and many are printed with either soy- or vegetable-based ink, which emits fewer volatile organic compounds during the printing process than petroleum-based ink.

Library of Congress Cataloging-in-Publication Data

Madanes, Cloé.
    The secret meaning of money: how it binds together families in love, envy, compassion, or anger / by Cloé Madanes with Claudio Madanes. — 1st ed.
       p.   cm.
    Includes index.
    ISBN 1-55542-701-4
    1. Family—Economic aspects—United States. 2. Money—Social aspects—United States. 3. Money—United States—Psychological aspects. I. Madanes, Claudio. II. Title.
HQ536.M255 1994
306.3'4—dc20   94-20980
                                      CIP

FIRST EDITION
HB Printing   10 9 8 7 6 5 4 3 2 1   *Code 9477*

Contents

viii   Contents

Acknowledgments

We would like to express heartfelt thanks to our editor, Alan Rinzler, for his encouragement, advice, and enthusiasm. Our special appreciation goes also to the staff and trainees at the Family Therapy Institute who were the therapists in the fictionalized case anecdotes presented in this book. They are Richard Belson, Edwin Child, Ricardo Chouhy, David Eddy, Tony Fasnmeyer, Luis Goncalvez, Lisa Hatcher, Helen Coale Lewis, Marcha Ortiz, and Neil Schiff.

To Magali and Mark

Chapter One

Introduction: The Challenge of Money

This book is about how we use money covertly in our struggles for power with our husbands, wives, parents, or children. We express our desires, our yearning for commitment, and our need for revenge and retribution through money. This secret power of money binds us together—brothers and sisters, young and old—in love, envy, compassion, and anger.

In our families, we use money as a secret weapon in manipulating a myriad of underlying, unresolved conflicts about sex, love, and power. Money can be given only to be taken away, promised but never fulfilled, withheld then granted beyond expectation. Financial problems are often the tip of an iceberg, concealing deeper, hidden issues between family members. Money can also be the issue underlying other conflicts over love and justice.

The Money in Our Lives

Everyone worries about money. Some of us feel that if only we could have more money, our lives would be greatly improved and we could find happiness. Yet those who have a great deal of money seem constantly worried about making more, how to spend it, and the possibility of losing it. Everyone worries about money, and no one seems satisfied with how much they have and how they use it.

The problems of the poor are very different from the problems of the wealthy, yet the family conflicts caused by how money is used may be quite similar across socioeconomic classes. For most of us, money is so intertwined with our lives that issues about money affect our health, intimate relationships, and relationships with our children and parents. Money ruins our digestion; money is on our mind when we have sex. It is an ever-present issue.

What Is Money?

Money is not just currency, not just that which allows us to acquire material possessions. With money we can also buy education, health, safety. We can buy time to enjoy beauty, art, the company of friends, adventure. With money we can help those whom we love and ensure that our children will have better opportunities. With money we can buy goods and services and also store that capacity for a future time or for future generations. Money is an instrument of justice with which we can do reparation to those we have harmed. A fair distribution of money within a family and society ensures equal opportunity to all. Money can be a metaphor for all the good things in life: material possessions, education, health, beauty, entertainment, love, and justice.

Yet, just as we know all the good things that money represents, so everyone is familiar with the problems it causes. Financial woes can lead to overwhelming distress. Even wealth often appears to be cursed, bringing with it more misery than joy. Many of us experience most intense despair about not making enough money and the fear of what might become of us or our children without it. Money can be a metaphor not only for all the good things in life but also for the root cause of all our problems.

Everyone realizes that money is an important cause of happiness or distress, yet there is a universal taboo with regard to talking about one's personal relationship to money in most social situations. It is considered in poor taste to talk about what things cost or someone's salary or wealth. So money is often not a subject addressed explicitly between parents and children, husbands and wives, brothers and sisters, good friends, or even therapist and patient.

Nevertheless, money is at the basis of marital and family life. Husband and wife, parent and child, brother and sister can fight bitterly over money. Parents often don't know how to talk about money with their children, how to give it, or when to withhold it, and husbands and wives argue about how much to help each of their children. Many who have divorced have learned bitterly that marriage is about money. That is the tie that is so difficult to break.

Money is a form of energy, the moving force of our civilization. This situation is a recent development in the history of humankind; it has not always been so. In the past the energy that sustained human transactions has been land, or livestock, or human slaves, or a natural substance such as water, salt, iron, or weapons. Yet even though people have always put their main energy into one thing or form, none of these became the immense mechanism that is money, the one thing that penetrates into every aspect of human life and that constitutes the chief element of contemporary culture. Today money is the energy that moves the world.

Money as Dirty

Freud was the first to recognize that money holds a secret meaning, but he only saw the negative side. To him, money symbolized excrements, with disgusting and despicable connotations. Perhaps this is why money is not a polite subject of conversation in most social situations.

Freud rebelled against the hypocrisy of institutionalized religion of the Victorian era with its condemnation of what was considered the "baser" part of human nature: the body, sexuality, and material desires. He lifted the taboo against thinking about sex as an important part of human life. But he did not do the same for money, perhaps because he believed that the desire for money is not an original, infantile desire; perhaps because in Freud's time money had not yet become the overpowering source of energy that it is today, the one symbol that represents all desires.

The taboo against giving money its place in our understanding of human nature remains. Even therapists, who do not hesitate to address every possible issue related to sex and power, have rarely addressed issues about money. They have hardly produced any words of wisdom about how to deal with money as an important part of the development of the person. Most people don't even think of consulting a therapist when they are plagued by financial conflicts. Yet probably more marriages break up because of disagreements about money than any other reason. Resentments about the way money is handled are probably the single most important issue that separates parent and child, brother and sister.

Money Gone Wrong

Depending on how money is used, it can be a symbol for love or for violence. Money can be offered and accepted as an expression of love, or it can be withheld or rejected as an expression of violence. The problem is complicated because violence involves not only physical pain but also intrusiveness, domination, control, and taking advantage of others. Love and violence are part of a continuum on which one frequently leads to the other.

At what point does a loving relationship that is possessive and overbearing become intrusive and controlling in a violent way? To what extent are people tied to one another in ways that are violent but stronger than the bond of love? The issue is aggravated by the struggle for material cravings and its common denominator: money.

The dilemma is further complicated because there are two kinds of people in the world: the Donald Trumps and the Mother Teresas. The Donald Trumps want things for themselves. Everything is to be accumulated, saved, invested for their own profit. They want all the wealth, power, sex, love, beauty, and fun that they can possibly get.

"I don't do it for the money," writes Trump. "I've got enough, much more than I'll ever need. I do it to do it. Deals are my art form."[1]

The Donald Trumps are not focused on giving to others, which makes it difficult to love and admire them. It seems that the more they want, the more they get and the more they are disliked.

The Mother Teresas also want wealth and power and material possessions, but they want to give it to others. They can be as driven as the Donald Trumps, but they crave not for themselves—they crave to give. The more they give, however, the more they may be open to criticism. Unsavory motivations are often attributed to the generous person because generosity can provoke envy rather than gratitude. We all secretly wish to be unselfish and giving, and watching those traits in another person can make us jealous.

Most of us are a mixture of Donald Trump and Mother Teresa. We want to take a lot and give a little, or we are Mother Teresas to our own family and Donald Trumps toward the rest of the world. Yet, for the purpose of this book, thinking in polarities will help us clarify who we are and what we truly want.

Money and Spirituality

In today's world money is what salvation was for the Middle Ages. The most important Holy Wars of the twentieth century are about money, not religion. Yet the question remains: Is there a place for spirituality in our modern conception of people? And if so, how does spirituality relate to money?

Spirituality is rarely a subject of discussion among those who attempt to regulate our economic activity. In the social sciences, the subject of spirituality is equally absent, perhaps because of the influence of Freudian ideas. In reacting against the repression it promoted, Freud discarded religion, and with it some of us lost track of the importance of spirituality for human life. Yet, in order to understand ourselves, we need to be in touch not only with our animal nature but also with our spiritual aspirations.[2]

In the past, organized religion regulated the discrimination between our spiritual obligations and our material desires. As spirituality disappeared as an element of the self, material desire began more and more to define our sense of identity. Desires then became cravings and addictions. An important balance was broken, and materialism went out of control.

Today money is the chief representation of the material world, of the "lower" world whose roots are in our physical needs, bodies, desires, and fears. Spirituality represents transcendence and compassion, the "higher" world of the search for meaning, oneness, and community.

Humans are two-natured beings in whom materialism and spirituality coexist. The struggle between these two natures is represented in the works of all the great spiritual leaders. All have taught that spirituality must be based on living normally in the material world. Buddhists, Christians, and Jews, among others, developed norms to regulate economic activity so that each individual would strive to satisfy not only his or her own needs but also those of the community. This is the idea in the Middle Way of Buddhism, the concept of "love thy neighbor" in Christianity, and the mitzvah in Judaism. The history of humankind can be described as a struggle between the forces of selfish materialism and the voice of justice and compassion.

Consequently, money can also be one of the elements that makes possible the expression of spirituality. It allows us to exercise compassion, to do justice, to "love our neighbor." But the hording of money of selfish purpose is contradictory with spiritual values. Where do we draw the line between the love of self and the love of others? To answer this question is to solve the dilemma between our two natures.

Created Wants

The idea that desire does not become less urgent the more it is satisfied seems contrary to common sense. Yet who is to say that the pain experienced from the deprivation of an intense desire for a skiing vacation is not worse than the pain of hunger? Probably the nature of human beings is such that when basic needs are satisfied, new needs appear.

We not only strive to satisfy our desires but also seem to seek the creation of new objects of desire. In The Affluent Society, economist John Kenneth Galbraith[3] points out that this aspect of our economic order is one of the chief factors that distinguishes it from all other economies in history. "One cannot defend production as satisfying wants if that production creates the wants," he writes.

"Production only fills a void that it has itself created. . . . It is the process of satisfying wants that creates the wants. . . . [T]he individual who urges the importance of production to satisfy these wants is precisely in the position of the onlooker who applauds the efforts of the squirrel to keep abreast of the wheel that is propelled by his own efforts."

Galbraith goes on to say that economists have failed to focus on the importance of modern want creation. Wants are still thought of as independently determined, and so the economists continue to seek unquestioningly the means to fulfill these wants. He says that the blindness of economists is similar to that of "a humanitarian who was long ago persuaded of the grievous shortage of hospital facilities in the town. He continues to importune the passers-by for money for more beds and refuses to notice that the town doctor is deftly knocking over pedestrians with his car to keep up the occupancy."

When creating new desires, we also create new conflicts. In Stephen King's[4] novel *Needful Things*, a demon comes to a small town in Maine and opens a store. He sells objects that have been specifically created to satisfy the innermost secret desires of each of the town's people. Each person recognizes an object as directed to satisfying a profound need, even though the need never existed before the person laid eyes on the object. A man sees a fishing rod exactly like the one his beloved father used to have. A woman finds a picture of Elvis Presley that can carry her to orgasmic ecstasy. A gambler buys a toy that predicts what horse will win at the races. The demon refuses to take money for these objects. He prefers to "dicker," but in dickering, the life of each person is compromised and they lose everything.

King's demon creates needful things, similar to Galbraith's "demons" who create artificial needs. But those demons are not the devil, nor are they the factories that produce objects that awaken desires we did not have before we knew of those objects' existence. The demons are inside us; they represent desire out of control, cravings to satisfy needs whose satisfaction creates new cravings.

In today's society, money, the energy that moves the world, is the currency that represents all of those cravings. The craving for money represents the need for a Porsche, not just a car as a means of transportation; for a vacation home, not just a dwelling; for cakes and cookies, not just food. The craving for money is an artificial need that represents all other artificial needs: the need to be thin and beautiful instead of simply healthy and strong, the need to be powerful and admired instead of simply gainfully employed, the need to communicate meaningfully instead of simply having good times.

All these are artificial needs, and the symbolic craving for money represents the craving for all these things. To obtain these things we dicker with our bodies, time, love, and peace of mind.

Scope of the Book

This book presents some guidelines for using money wisely in couples and families. Stories from my own experience and work as a therapist are told to reveal complicated problems in which money, sex, power, and love are interconnected. These stories show how to solve specific money problems and also how to approach many difficulties that may not appear to be related to financial issues but can be resolved by using money wisely.

Those who have a great deal of money as well as those who have very little can benefit from understanding how the financial resources that are available to them or their families can be used to bring about happiness and prevent pain. This book is based in the belief that people can use their own strengths to solve problems. Money is one of those strengths.

The book will explain how to understand and resolve specific problems in which money is a metaphor for other underlying issues about love and power. But money is not only a metaphor. Sometimes money is itself the underlying issue in what appear to be other conflicts over love and justice. The book will also address this issue.

My hope in writing this book is to increase our knowledge of how we relate to money and all the cravings that money represents. The book does not present simple solutions and will not help you achieve financial success. Instead, we will look at the delicate balance between our individual needs and our desire to give to those we love. We will examine how issues about money can elicit deep conflicts. We will analyze how relationships can get stuck around money issues and how to get them unstuck. We will see how our behavior can provoke and maintain the behavior of others and how we can use ourselves to bring about change.

Since the subject of money touches almost every aspect of our social life, I have had to make some choices. Consequently, I have focused largely on the family. Our deepest love is to our children, spouses, parents, lovers, and siblings. Relationships with family are our primary and most significant ones. They are the greatest source of happiness and misery. These difficult relationships are the ones that we often cannot change no matter how hard we try. If we can understand our true needs as opposed to our created wants, we will know how to use money wisely within the family, and we will deal with money and material possessions with greater clarity and confidence in other social situations.

Getting the Most Out of This Book

Read the whole book. If you are single, you will still find that the chapters on marriage are useful. Even though you may be young, read the chapters on older couples. The book is about money and relationships, and you will find that you can apply the ideas to all kinds of relationships in your life. As you read, transfer what you are learning to your own particular situation.

The book will help you understand issues about money and family life and use money more wisely by developing your skills in three areas:

1. Understanding what money and material possessions mean to you and to your family, including:
    a. What is the secret meaning of money in your family?
    b. What and how much do you want?
    c. Why do you want it?
    d. Is it for yourself or to give to others?
    e. Who owes whom?
    f. Who is responsible for what?
        These are complicated questions to answer. You may find that you are trapped putting all your energy into objectives that are not your own. You may be trying to satisfy the cravings of somebody else in your family, not your own cravings. You may find that you are taking responsibilities that are not yours to take or that you are not truly grateful when you should be. You may find that you want to do more for others or that you are already doing too much.
2. Speaking openly about money. This skill will improve the chances that your opinion will count and that you will resolve conflicts and disagreements. You will be able to break the taboos and family rules against addressing money issues explicitly. In understanding all that money represents, you will know when it is better to respect the taboo and not to talk about money.
3. Thinking more clearly about money. Reading about how other people think will help you clarify how you are similar or different. In understanding others, you will understand yourself. In realizing that others think about money and use it quite differently from you, you will increase your range of choices. You'll learn how your behavior affects others and how you can use money to improve relationships. As you appreciate how money

is the root cause for many problems in your family, you'll be able to do something about it.

In the chapters that follow, we will look at the strong anxiety associated with the secret meaning of money. We'll discuss many examples of how to handle your own anxiety and guilt, as well as the anxiety and guilt of those you love. The book will help you think more clearly about the covert meaning of money in your life, about your choices, and about how to make better decisions. You will not only learn new ways of handling money but also acquire a stronger sense of self.

Many difficulties in life occur when we choose between having money and having love. This book will show you how you can have both.

Chapter Two

Money and the Young Couple

When thinking about money and the family, we must begin with how money issues are handled at the origin of family life—with the young couple. They are Adam and Eve, the creators of the family. The secret meaning of money, and all that money represents, can play a very prominent role in the earliest conflicts of the young couple.

As we become young adults, it's not always easy to make a long-term relationship work. On the one hand, we want to be separate and independent. We don't always want to subordinate our goals to the needs of another person. We don't want to make the transition from "mine" to "ours." We don't want to share. We don't want to give.

On the other hand, we want to be loved and appreciated. We want intimacy. We want to be necessary to the well-being of our partner. Yet we want to succeed as individuals; we want to win, to be the best. How can we do this if not at the expense of our spouse? How can we have intimacy and love while we are striving to achieve our individual goals instead of selflessly offering love and support?

For a marital relationship to be successful, it must be based on collaboration, not competition. But for many young people marriage is the first relationship that is supposed to be collaborative and not competitive. When we are young, we are expected to take as much as we can from our parents, teachers, relatives, and community. We are expected to compete with our peers at school, in sports, and on the job. It's no wonder that the shift to collaboration with a lover or spouse is so difficult to make.

The story of Megan and Larry, a young couple who sought my help, is about changing from competition to collaboration. The content of their battles may be different from yours, but their patterns of interaction are almost universal to young couples. They were caught in a vicious cycle in which each provoked the other to behave in unfortunate ways.

Getting Versus Giving

Megan called me to make an appointment. "I have a problem with my husband," she said in a childish, whining voice. "He talks about an old girlfriend all the time, and it's making me crazy. Also I've had this fear of gaining weight all my life. When I eat something fattening, I make myself throw up."

"This is a problem of desire," I thought. "The husband wants another woman. She wants food but also a thin figure."

Megan's problem is common in young couples: the fear of being unattractive to the mate (Megan's fear), a confusion about appropriate physical needs (the desire for food in young women is often a metaphor for sexual cravings or a desire to be loved), and the difficulty in coming to terms with the fact that in choosing one spouse one has given up mating with anyone else (apparently a problem of Megan's husband).

When I met Megan, I was impressed by her beauty: blonde, blue-eyed, small but athletic, she was the prototype of the all-American girl, the cheerleader.

Pouting and with her little girl's voice, she said, "Larry used to talk to me about his old girlfriend before. But he used to say, 'She's not my type; she's not athletic; she doesn't work out. I hate how she used to shop.' But now he can't see anything negative about her. Now she really looks like power and money. All of a sudden he's in this marriage, and we don't have any money, so she stands for carefree fun. This girl was rich. Her parents had said to Larry, 'If you marry Darlene, we'll give you a Porsche.' I said to him, 'There's just not that kind of dowry where I come from, I'm sorry! It just didn't come with the package.' And I feel so sad because it's really not my inadequacy. It's not what I don't have—it's all that her parents can give her."

Megan began to cry as she added, "And he says all this to me just when I'm preparing my final exams."

Apparently Megan was about to graduate from an excellent college while Larry had barely finished high school. He was hoping to make it big with his rock and roll band. I turned to him and asked, "Do you do this to provoke her when she is just about to have the big success of finishing college?"

"Provoking is kind of a harsh thing to say," said Larry. "I don't think it's her success that started me talking about these things, dreaming about these things I've done in the past. This isn't abnormal for me. I've done this before, even before I met Megan. I often withdraw into myself, thinking about old girlfriends and stuff like that, questioning things like 'God! Why did I break up with Darlene! Did I do the right thing?'"

Larry's manner was definitely provocative. He insisted, "It might happen again. I don't go out and plan this stuff and say, 'Hey, I think I'll do this tomorrow!'"

I said to Larry, "Perhaps it is difficult for you to tolerate Megan's success. Few men are strong enough that they can tolerate having a wife who is more educated and perhaps more successful than they are. You look like someone strong enough to tolerate your wife's success, but I'm not sure. When she graduates from college, she might even make more money than you."

"I can't wait," said Larry. "The day she starts making money is the day we're going to be financially free, you know. That's all I'm waiting for. I'm not trying to keep her suppressed; I'm not trying to put her down or to threaten her. It's just the way I am. It has to do with feelings that are inside of me."

Megan said, "What kind of feelings?"

"Just anger, and, you know, depression, and frustration."

"About what?"

"About me not being, you know, just feeling like I'm stuck in a rut."

Megan said, "He's upset about my vomiting, and he also got real upset about the whole thing about sex. The other day he said, 'Can we have sex now?' I said, 'Can we wait till later? Do you ever think . . .' To me, I get really sore; I can't go four or five times like he wants to. And he said some really hurtful things about that other girl, how she never said no."

Megan's tone had become more and more whining, and her eyes filled with tears. "'I don't reject you, Larry,' I said. 'Did you ever think it's a two-way street? Sure, I could always do it just to satisfy you!' Lately he hasn't worried about me, about how to satisfy me. It's more like he just worries about himself."

Megan then talked about how before they were married, Larry had worked in a gay bar, and now he was threatening to go back to that job. She said, "He said to me that he might want to dance again. He said, 'I don't think I ever would, but I got the thought. It crossed my mind." She looked at my puzzled face and added, "He used to dance. He used to be a stripper."

"He did?" I said, unable to hide my shock. "How old was he then?"

"I'm not sure. He did it for about four months. He was making great money. He said he was not a stripper because he would go down to a little G-string, right, Larry? And the other weird thing is that he got the job through his uncle. But he has a value system, and he was questioning his value system. He really felt, 'This is not Larry.' He felt like, sure, this is an ego boost, but it was strange because he was dancing in a gay bar. These clean-cut boys that are straight just turn the gay men wild. You know what I mean? He made all the tips. He could walk away and feel a little weird about it but still go home with the money and feel content. I don't think he questioned his sexuality."

"Come on!" said Larry, embarrassed. "It was just a way of making very good money."

Money was as important to Larry as food was to Megan. She was willing to go to the extreme of making herself vomit for the pleasure of eating. He was willing to go to the extreme of dancing in a gay bar for the satisfaction of making money.

The Balance of Power

What were Megan and Larry doing to each other? What part did money, and all the cravings that money stands for, play in their relationship?

Larry tormented Megan with his desire for money. He missed his former girlfriend because she represented money. He would not show affection to Megan and could not stop thinking about the money he could have if he were involved with another woman.

Megan withheld sex from him and did not even let him have food in the house, for fear that she would be tempted to eat it. Both Megan and Larry were focused on wanting, on getting, and had great difficulty in giving. This is typical of the difficulties of many young couples, as well as others who are not so young.

Another problem Megan and Larry had was that they were so focused on their economic troubles, on their quarrels and fears, that they had lost their ability to have fun together.

Worse than this, a major problem for the young couple was the competition between them. The difference in their education was an issue. Megan was about to graduate with very good grades from an excellent college. Larry had only a high school education.

Megan's vomiting expressed not only her problems with desire. It was also a way to put herself down and build Larry up. Megan seemed to go out of her way to present herself as childish. She pouted and always talked with the voice of a little girl. She appeared to be afraid that if she behaved like a competent, mature woman, Larry would feel inferior and leave her.

In fact, Megan was frequently jealous, particularly when Larry was away playing with his band. She often insisted on going with him to keep an eye on the "groupies" that gathered around him. She would sit listening to the band and crying in a way that was sometimes so disturbing that he had to stop playing to comfort her.

In talking about how he wanted a woman with money, Larry was expressing his fear about whether he could make enough money to keep Megan in the marriage or whether she would move beyond him, surpass him, and perhaps find a man who had money. He was questioning his own self-worth, while Megan, like most young wives, wanted her husband to help her with her own feelings of inadequacy.

Larry responded to Megan's accomplishments at school like many young husbands do. Although ostensibly happy with her success, he feared that she would not need him any longer, so he provoked her back to the disturbed behavior and feelings of inadequacy that made him feel superior and needed. But when he was needed, he couldn't really give to Megan. He could only think about what he wanted and couldn't have because of Megan.

It was no coincidence that as Megan was about to graduate and was feeling good about herself, Larry started thinking about past relationships, money, and sex—all the things that are tempting. He even brought home a cake that his mother baked, when he could have said, "Thanks, Mom, but I can't take it home." (His mother knew about Megan's constant dieting.) When Megan ate the cake and vomited, Larry became the winner. She had self-destructed; he was competent and on top of the situation.

Megan and Larry were at war, in a struggle for power.

Fears and Inadequacies

Megan and Larry were trapped in a relationship that was more like a competition than a collaboration. Why were they at war with each other? What were their battles really about? Were they truly about the former rich girlfriend, about making money as a stripper, about vomiting? What fears, what sense of inferiority was driving them to fight with one another?

Each wanted so much from the other, yet they were both so unwilling to give. Each wanted love, money, security, self-esteem, and each wanted the other to provide all those things. Each secretly envied the other spouse and felt inferior and inadequate.

Yet both were reluctant to be the first one to give, in order to elicit a better response. This lack of collaboration and the competition between them led each to feel empty and even more needy for the love, money, security, and self-esteem they desperately wanted.

Some couples fight constantly about money: who should make it, how it should be spent, who should pay the bills. Other couples fight about the wants that money represents, the needful things, the artificial necessities.

This was the case with Megan and Larry. They argued about food (or the vomiting of food), the Porsche and rich girlfriend, and the money that could be made as a stripper. Through these arguments they expressed the fear that each would not be able to give enough to the other, that they would not be able to hold on to the other, and that they would not be able to succeed in life.

Ending the War

I did many different things to help Megan and Larry. I gave them suggestions and coaxed them to be nicer to one another. I attributed good intentions to each and redefined their negative behaviors so they would appear well intentioned. I saw each separately, but most of the time I met with them together. I spent a great deal of time making sure that I understood each one's point of view.

I told Megan and Larry that the first goal of therapy would be to help them recover the ability to have fun together. I asked them to make a list of all the fun things they could possibly do together in the next month, the next year, and the next five years. They were to do one thing from that list each week.

I suggested that few men are strong enough to tolerate having a wife who is more educated or more successful than they are. If Megan gave up her obsession with food, she would no longer have a handicap, and perhaps Larry would not be able to tolerate that. I thought that Larry was actually man enough to tolerate having a successful wife, but I wasn't sure. Larry said he certainly could tolerate it and would like nothing better than for Megan to be successful.

I talked with each spouse about the things they most needed. Megan said she needed not to have fattening foods in the house. Larry complained bitterly about his hunger. I suggested that Larry pick one food that Megan would agree she could tolerate. They agreed on cheese.

Megan, like most young wives, wanted her husband to help her with her feelings of inadequacy, instead of wanting to be with him for their mutual enjoyment. I asked her to show him that she needed him for better reasons, for example, for sex. I suggested that in between each time that he asked her for sex, she approach him sexually to show that she needed him too.

I asked Larry to smother Megan with affection, since that was what she always craved, but to do it sometimes when he knew that she didn't want to be bothered. In this way, Megan might get some idea for how Larry felt when she demanded attention at times when he was busy.

I noticed that every time that Megan was successful or had something important to do, Larry provoked her into her inadequate behaviors. I used a paradoxical approach to change Larry's behavior. Instead of telling him to stop provoking Megan, which would not have worked since his behavior was quite out of his awareness, I decided to approach him indirectly. I asked him to plan a provocation deliberately, so Megan would know ahead of time and not be taken by surprise. My expectation was that Larry would react against deliberately provoking Megan and therefore not provoke her.

As I expected, Larry did not want to provoke his wife deliberately to make her unhappy. He said that he couldn't even think of how to provoke her deliberately. I suggested that he could have his mother over for dinner and that Megan should cook. Larry loved the idea. Megan said, "Just having to talk to her on the phone provokes me." But she accepted the plan because it meant that Larry would not provoke her in any other way that week.

The young couple reported later that the dinner went very well. For a long time there were no further provocations from Larry. Megan had done something generous toward someone Larry loved, an unusual event since it was so particularly difficult for her to be giving.

Relating This Story to Your Problems

Some of the interventions that worked for Megan and Larry can be used to resolve your own difficulties with your spouse around money and all those wants that money represents.

Couples are usually attracted to one another because of the fun they have together. But eventually they begin to focus on their problems, quarrels, and fears, and they lose the ability to have fun. Having fun is an essential part of marriage and must be recovered.

You and your spouse can make a list of all the fun things that you can possibly do together in the next month, the next year, and the next five years. You can read the list to each other. When discussing the list, emphasize the joy that you have had in one another and all the wonderful things that you can still do together.

Few people are strong enough that they can tolerate having a mate who is more accomplished and successful than they are. The successful spouse, afraid of being rejected, often develops a weakness of character or an incapacitating habit that will compensate for his or her superiority in other areas. The less successful spouse can then feel at least partially superior. If the more successful spouse eventually gives up the handicap, it becomes once more apparent how competent and successful he or she is, and perhaps the other spouse will not be able to tolerate that success. It is crucial in a marriage to divide areas of expertise so that each can be successful in their own way.

Steps Toward Solutions

A young couple can follow four steps to overcome their difficulties. Although not all these steps involve dealing directly with money or needful things, each step represents the preparation necessary for dealing with these issues.

The order of the steps may vary and does not need to be followed in the same way by every couple. A couple can decide together to change their relationship and take each step until they are successful. Even one spouse alone can follow the steps and change the relationship. When one person changes, the interaction changes, and the other person also has to change.

Encourage Fun and Reassurance

Each spouse has to make the shift from needing the other because of their own inadequacies, to wanting to be with the other because of the enjoyment and pleasure derived from the relationship. That is, the couple has to make the shift from wanting to be together because each helps the other with their difficulties to wanting to be together because they enjoy one another.

There are different ways of doing this. An obvious one is to increase the good times spent together, while acknowledging to one another that the relationship is important because of these good times.

One can say, for example, "I don't care if we ever make money, I enjoy so much doing things with you."

Or, "All week I put up with my job thinking about the fun I'm going to have with you in the weekend."

Another positive statement: "Maybe it is precisely because we like and need different things that we complement each other so well. We balance each other."

While increasing the intensity and frequency of good times together, the couple has to make an effort to complain less to one another and rely less on each other for comfort when they are anxious.

A wife can say to her husband, "When I feel like worrying about money, I call my girlfriend, but when I want to have a good time, I talk with you." The idea is for us to take care of ourselves or rely also on friends and relatives rather than to depend exclusively on our spouse.

Be Giving and Loving

Each spouse has to practice generosity both verbally and in action: praising the other person, expressing admiration for the spouse's work and accomplishments, giving presents, allowing the other to make decisions involving the family's finances or the children.

A successful marriage must be a combination of wanting to be loved, wanting to receive, and wanting to love the other, wanting to give. Each spouse needs to move from wanting to be loved and cared for to wanting to give their love, to care for the other person.

This is not an easy task. Each spouse has to make a practice every day of remembering that marriage is not just about receiving and that each must make an effort every day to give attention, consideration, recognition, material things, and love to the other person.

Shift from Poverty to Wealth

It is just as easy to focus on what one does have as it is to focus on what one does not have. The most treasured possessions of a couple are not necessarily measured in dollars. They are not necessarily material things. A couple must move away from an emphasis on what they desire to an appreciation of what they have. There has to be a shift from feelings of emptiness to feelings of self-worth, wealth, and richness. Both husband and wife need to change from a focus on what they want or what is missing, to a focus on what they do have, on the material and spiritual possessions that are theirs.

Move from Provocation to Play

Instead of responding to provocation by having a battle, it is best to respond to provocation as an indication to play. Certain kinds of arguments, particularly about money, can become so intense that they can lead to physical violence. Accusations, recriminations, and expressions of anxiety about money are provocations often leading to bitter fights. It is possible to respond instead with affection and humor.[1]

One way of doing this is for the husband to begin to take off his clothes when the wife becomes hostile. He can begin by taking off his tie, then his shirt, and then start unbuttoning his pants, whether he and his wife are in the middle of the street, or at home, or wherever they are. This tactic interrupts the interaction, and the message becomes "This is play."

For example, a young dentist and his wife had terrible arguments about money. She wanted to invest in stocks and bonds and set money aside in savings accounts. He wanted to reinvest in his practice, purchasing equipment and hiring more personnel. The wife constantly complained to the husband about how they were not setting aside enough money in their savings. At dinner parties with friends, when they were watching a movie, or simply walking down the street, anything would trigger her associations, and she would remind him that they were not saving any money. He responded with anger and embarrassment. The problem was ruining an otherwise very good relationship.

When they consulted me, I suggested a simple solution: to set aside one evening a week when they would go out to dinner together and talk about money. At no other times would they talk about money, only at those dinners. They began to do this, but even so the wife could not resist bringing up the subject in all kinds of other circumstances.

So I suggested that every time she brought up the subject, anywhere other than at the specified dinners, the husband should immediately begin to take off his clothes. He would begin unobtrusively perhaps by taking off his tie. If she continued talking, perhaps he would remove his belt or shoes, then he would continue with his shirt, and so on, even if he ended up completely naked. He would do this no matter where they were, on the street, at a party, or at home. He would stop removing his clothes only when she stopped talking about money. This would be a reminder to her that the subject of money could only be addressed once a week at their special dinner together.

The husband laughed at the idea, and the wife said, "You wouldn't dare to do it!"

"I certainly would," he said. And he did.

On several occasions when they were out with friends, he removed three or four items of clothing before she stopped alluding to their problems with money. At home she didn't stop until he was completely naked, then they both burst out laughing. Soon they were no longer arguing uncontrollably about money. The wife discovered that there was a funny, daring, exhibitionist aspect to the husband's personality that she had not been aware of and that was fun.

This method for changing interactions was inspired by studies that show how dogs, beavers, and other animals will exhibit a behavior that humans would usually identify as aggressive but animals can distinguish as actually playful. Dogs and other animals will fight in play without any hostile intent. Humans may have difficulty recognizing the difference, but the animals know.

Human interaction can be influenced in the same way so that instead of deteriorating into violence, it can shift to humor and play. So whenever possible, it is a good idea for couples to change provocation to hostility, to provocation to play.

Satisfying Our Needs

Megan and Larry were putting all their energy into fighting. Instead of collaborating to get ahead in life, they argued about their needs and deprivations: food, sex, money, former lovers. Each wanted to get as much as possible from the other and give as little as possible. Megan wanted Larry's unconditional support in having her way about food. Larry wanted Megan's unconditional support in having his way about sex. Each wanted to work as little as possible and for the other to provide whatever money was needed. Of course, most of us secretly want the same things: to satisfy our own needs and be unconditionally supported by our spouse. But maturity means to recognize that we have to give in order to receive.

It's difficult to accept the fact that we cannot expect others to satisfy our own needs and desires if we don't respond in kind. There is nothing wrong with *wanting* if wanting comes together with giving. Marriage is a quid pro quo in which we are not guaranteed that justice will prevail. At times we will give more than we receive. We can put an end to fighting only when we give up the idea that we should only be at the receiving end. When we focus on giving instead of receiving, on generosity instead of desire, we become free from depending on the other person. It is only then that we recover the power to act on our own behalf.

Our Difficult Parents

There are times when we all have to wonder, Where do these needs for money come from? Why do I have so much desire? Why do I always want more? Sometimes we have to search for the origin of our feelings of inadequacy and emptiness not in the relationship with our spouse but in our own childhoods. We might ask ourselves, How did I become so worried about money? Why do I have these cravings? Is it the wish to be loved? How did I get to feel so unloved or so easily humiliated? What happened to me in my childhood?

It is important to discuss early relationships with one's family of origin to discover what the problems were in those relationships. We need to explain ourselves to our spouse in relation to what happened to us in the past. This is the subject of the next chapter.

Chapter Three

Money and Our Difficult Parents

As we grow up, it is difficult to separate from our parents. This separation is a process that sometimes takes most of our adult life to complete. Often, when we finally feel we have truly separated from them, we discover that we must take care of our elderly parents and so we continue the struggle. There seems to be no separation, just changes in the relationship.

But what about those people who live far away from their parents and don't see them for years? Haven't they separated? Maybe so, but if they are still organizing their lives in opposition to their parents or to make a point to their parents, if they are still blaming their parents for everything that went wrong in their lives, then there has been no separation. No matter how much we try, it is very difficult to lose our parents. Even when they are dead, they continue to be present in our minds.

An invisible string ties parents and children together across time and distance. The string is even stronger when money is attached to it. Money is often a secret umbilical cord in the struggle of young adults for separation from their parents. Children use money covertly—how much they demand and what they do with it—to rebel and to exact retribution. Parents use money covertly—how much they give and what they want in exchange—to reject or to hold onto their children.

Making Our Parents Pay

Most of us have a tendency to blame our parents for everything that is wrong about us. If we are shy, afraid of failure, angry, overweight, or anxious, it must be because of something that our parents did to us in our childhood.

Why do we blame our parents? Do we truly believe that they deserve so much responsibility for our destiny? Is it just human nature to resent our parents? If we blame them for all our faults, why don't we give them credit for our virtues and successes?

Blaming our parents is a useful mechanism that helps us protect our current relationships. For most of us, the love of our parents is unconditional. We can attack and blame them knowing that eventually they'll forgive us and continue to love us. This is usually not true of our spouses, friends, and colleagues.

Consider this: If we did not find the cause of all our problems in our parents, we would have to look at our current relationships. But when a husband blames his wife for making him anxious, instead of his mother, the result may be a separation. And when a woman notices that her depression and fear of failure have to do with her competitive relationship with highly successful friends, she might lose those friendships. So it's easier to blame our parents and childhoods rather than risk losing our marriages, jobs, and social life.

The fact that blaming our parents is a helpful mechanism for living explains the success of all the self-help movements that emphasize the "inner child" or call us "adult children." These books and groups appeal to what we are already doing and already know: that by blaming our parents we not only protect ourselves from having to take responsibility for our own lives but we also protect our current relationships.

Yet sometimes not confronting our parents with the harm they have done to us is what keeps us from getting on with our lives. There are even situations when simply confronting our parents is not enough. We must also make them pay for how they've wronged us.

Some people come out of their childhoods like innocent victims of war crimes, and damages should be paid, even if only as a symbolic compensation for their suffering. Money can be used as reparation. When no money is available for damages, there can at least be apologies. Often a person cannot truly become an adult until the parents have recognized and apologized for the harm they have done.

Criminal Fathers

I met Kevin through his little girl. Their family therapist asked for a consultation with me because the child's problem was very serious and life threatening. She was diabetic, and her diabetes was out of control. The numerous doctors whom the parents had consulted thought her emotional instability was the cause of these frequent diabetic crises. Beatrice was only ten years old, yet she had been so upset that she had attempted to kill herself with an overdose of insulin.

Suicide threats and attempts are so rare at this age that I knew that Beatrice had to be acting out someone else's fantasies. There had to be someone else in the family who was covertly encouraging the suicide. That someone was probably a parent who believed that life was just too painful and not worth living.

As soon as I met Kevin, Beatrice's father, I knew it had to be him. One of the first things he said to me was, "I don't blame her for wanting to die. Living with a chronic illness is so difficult. In fact, the way she feels is almost like a replay of my own childhood. There were many times in my childhood when I wanted to die. And even now I am often depressed."

Talking with the family, I realized how worried Beatrice was about her father. Kevin was a musician who could not make a living with his music and refused to take any other career seriously. He occasionally held part-time jobs. As he described his difficulties, Beatrice looked at him with terrible sadness.

My first impression of Beatrice was that she adored her father and was driven to despair by his intense and frequent depressions. No matter how Beatrice was treated, something had to be done for her father or I would not succeed in helping her. It was her worry about her father that made her so emotional that her diabetes could not be controlled. In order to help her, I had to find out what was at the bottom of the father's depression.

I saw Kevin alone, suspecting that what he had to tell me was probably not for the children and maybe not even for his wife to hear. I said that I remembered that when we first met he had mentioned that he had had a very sad childhood and had even thought of killing himself. Why? What had happened to him in his childhood?

In a voice shaking with anxiety, he told me that he had been sexually abused by his father, from the age of five until adolescence. He had never told anyone. When his father died, he expected to inherit a large amount of money. Because of this expectation, he had never prepared for a career. He had never thought that he would have to work for a living. He would be rich, and somehow the inheritance would compensate for the pain his father had caused him.

When he found that there was no inheritance, he was certain that his mother had robbed him. He confronted her and did not believe it when she said that there was no inheritance, only debts. He had never told her about the abuse, but he blamed her for not having protected him from his father. Now he also blamed her for stealing from him. Consequently, since the funeral he and his mother had never spoken.

It's not uncommon in a well-to-do family for an abused child to look forward to an inheritance, hoping that it will somehow compensate for some of the pain from the abuse. But in order to be able to leave his childhood behind, Kevin had to tell his mother the truth about his father's behavior and find out from her what had really happened with the father's money. By not talking to his mother about the sexual abuse, he was still holding onto the secret that his father had coerced him to conceal. By not learning the truth about the money, he was still holding onto the dream that he was still a child who didn't need to work or have a family to support.

Had Kevin's father been alive, I would have confronted him about the abuse and insisted that he do reparation to Kevin for the crime he had inflicted. But the man was dead. The best I could do was to confront the mother and see whether she could perform any reparation.

With difficulty, I convinced Kevin to let me invite his mother to meet with us so we could find out whether she knew how her son was being victimized. I told him that I also would facilitate a discussion about the money in the family.

The mother accepted the invitation without hesitation and flew six hours to our appointment. She said that she could never understand why Kevin was so angry at her. I told her about how he had been sexually abused by his father through his childhood. She was shocked, and cried, saying that she had never suspected it. I asked her to apologize to Kevin for not having protected him from his father, for not having suspected, imagined, or even noticed the signs that her son was disturbed and suffering. She apologized sincerely, saying that she not only would have divorced the father but would also have put him in jail.

I then addressed the issue of the money, and she proved to Kevin that she lived in poverty because the father had left nothing but debts. During his life, she had been tyrannized by him. She had never had any power over the money that he made and spent. Mother and son cried when she said that he was all she had in life, and she had lost him. They reconciled, and Beatrice and her sister had a grandmother for the first time.

Kevin improved slowly over a period of months, letting go of his depression as he recovered his relationship with his mother and as he realized that he could no longer expect either pain or financial gain from his father. Whatever would become of him, he would have to do it on his own. Kevin was able to become an adult and a competent father to his children because his mother recognized the harm that was done to him and the fact that she had failed to protect him. If he had been able to confront his father before his death, if he had insisted on reparation by the father for his crime, Kevin would have saved himself a great deal of anguish. His children would have had a better father; his wife, a better husband.[1]

Beatrice improved steadily. Months later, when her diabetes was under control, she sent me a little note saying how happy she was to see that her father was doing better. The child was able to go on with life and make the best of her situation because the father was able to do the same.

Damages

Fortunately, most of us have not been sexually abused by our fathers, but many have suffered physical abuse and neglect. In such cases, it's important to our own well-being and that of our children that we confront our parents and demand reparation, that we are paid damages so to speak.

Just as it's important for justice to prevail in our social organization, so it's important for justice to prevail in our family systems. When we are survivors of a crime, keeping it secret makes us not only victims but accomplices. When the secret is revealed, the abusive parent is often punished by society through its penal system. But that punishment is not enough—there has to be a punishment from the family.

That punishment must involve reparation to the victim. The act of reparation, of paying damages, is the beginning of change in the relationship between parents and children. It sets the example for future generations to be giving and loving instead of cruel and punitive.

Secrets

Beatrice's family had sexual secrets and money secrets. The two are often related. When there are sexual violations and improprieties in a family, one can reasonably suspect that there are financial violations and improprieties that are equally serious.

When husband and wife are cheating each other sexually, they are often also cheating each other financially. If a parent is abusing a child sexually, often financial crimes and abuse exist in the family as well.

Money and sex are related in complex ways. Violations in one of these areas of life seem to appear at the same time as violations in the other area. Perhaps the reason is that when a basic code of ethics is broken in one area, the whole ethical structure of family life breaks. That is why financial transgressions come together not only with sexual violations but also with violence, lying, and cheating in other areas.

Taking Care of Our Parents

Humans are the only animals that take care of their parents. We begin life totally unable to take care of ourselves and completely dependent on our parents. Gradually we must make the transition to becoming equal to them. And eventually we must take care of our parents as they become incapacitated to look after themselves. This process is probably the most difficult transition in a person's life. It is the transition from having all our needs met by our parents to meeting all the needs of our parents.

For many people, the most difficult years are during adolescence and young adulthood. At this time most of us become fully aware of the fact that we are becoming stronger and more competent than our parents. It's then that our need to feel appreciated and respected seems greater. We crave to be heard. We have strong opinions and want to give advice, particularly to our parents. For a young person to make the successful transition to adult life, parents must show appreciation and respect and even be willing to listen to the young person's advice. They must be willing to accept their children's love and support.

It is very difficult for a young person to make the transition into adulthood when the parents are perfectly competent, independent, and in control of their lives. When parents are highly accomplished in every area of their lives, children feel that they will never achieve the same and, what is more important, that they are not needed, that they will never be able to take care of their parents.

Good Intentions

Even though emotionally independent parents are difficult, the transition to adult life is even more difficult when parents have depended on the emotional support of their children very early in their lives. It is difficult to become an adult when one has not had a childhood.

This was Megan's situation. In the previous chapter we left her when she was inviting her mother-in-law to dinner.

Both Megan and Larry were only children, they had no brothers or sisters. Larry's father had abandoned the family when he was a child, and his mother had been depressed and on medication for most of her life. Larry had no doubt that most of his problems stemmed from his parents and not from his relationship with Megan. Megan was the child of well-to-do middle-class parents. She had been born with a club foot and had suffered operations, casts, and various devices through her childhood. During this time, she had slept in her parents' bed at night because they worried so much about her. She had continued to sleep with them until the age of twelve, when she finally moved to another room at her own insistence. Shortly thereafter the parents separated.

Megan was wild and out of control as an adolescent, although she always managed to get good grades in school. She ran away to New York when she was seventeen, and eventually she was admitted to college. Her mother gave her some financial support. When trouble developed in Megan's marriage, it was the mother who financed the therapy.

Megan's mother had become a successful businesswoman after her divorce. When I heard that she was coming to town, I asked Megan to bring her to my office. I said to Megan that most of her problems originated with her parents, not with Larry, and I asked her permission to be frank with her mother.

Megan's mother, Janet, was attractive and youthful, although too heavily made up. Her very black hair and false eyelashes gave a certain dramatic starkness to her features. She seemed nervous about meeting me but was extremely cordial and open to my questions.

"Why did Megan sleep with you and your husband for the first twelve years of her life?" I asked.

In my twenty-five years of experience as a therapist I had never encountered this situation. The fact that Megan lived an almost normal life, that she was able to marry and about to graduate from college, and that her intelligence seemed quite intact, speaks to the resiliency of human beings.

She laughed nervously and said, "The sad fact about it—and this is the honest truth—I didn't think anything of it. I know it looks sick and weird, but it didn't seem sick and weird at the time because we all loved one another so much."

Janet told about her suffering as she watched Megan's pain during her early childhood. She broke into tears. "She got the cast when she was only five weeks old! I loved her so much, and when I think of the pain she experienced. . . . No child should have to experience that pain. She had to overcome so much!"

Janet talked about what a beautiful child Megan had been. She said that after she divorced she didn't want to date anyone because she was afraid that they would be attracted to Megan and do something sexual to her.

I said, "This reminds me that Megan told me that after the divorce, her father came home drunk one night, confused her with his girlfriend, and fondled her. Did you know about that?"

"No," said Janet.

"I thought I told you," said Megan. "He pulled me into his sleeping bag and was touching me all over. I could hardly get out of his vise. It was the most . . . ," she shuddered.

"That's horrible," said the mother.

I asked, "Do you think this might have happened when she was younger also?"

"I'm not naive by any means," said Janet. "I'm sure that if this had happened when she was a child, I would have noticed something."

"I would like you to apologize to Megan for not having protected her, even though I know you weren't there at the time and
it was after the divorce," I said.

"At that age, how old were you? Sixteen, seventeen?" asked
Janet.

Megan said, "I ran the streets since I was nine or ten. If I was
at his house, it was beyond the point where she could do anything."

"She was a strong, free spirit," interrupted her mother. "I didn't
know how I could have prevented it. But I certainly apologize for
her even having to see her father like that. I can't believe it—he
was such a caring father. But now I've seen that after the divorce
he never gave her any financial support whatsoever. If you love
somebody that much, you find a way to help that person; you have
a responsibility."

"You're right," I said. This was the opportunity I was waiting
for. Janet had spontaneously said that when you love somebody,
you find a way to help that person financially. I had met with her
not only to ask her to apologize to Megan for the many things she
had done wrong but also to enlist her financial help as a way of paying reparation to her daughter.

Janet continued, "If *I* could get ahead financially, surely he
could have helped her a little bit. Just the fact that he didn't have
any more responsibility surprised me. For this to happen, it makes
me sick inside; it makes me want to throw up."

Megan said, "That's exactly the feeling. Makes you want to
throw up."

Now I understood the meaning of Megan's problem with vomiting. She was throwing up with disgust at her father in whose bed
she had slept for the first twelve years of her life, who had
attempted to abuse her sexually, and who had refused her emotional and financial support.

I said, "Tell Megan that you would have wanted to protect her
and that you're sorry that you didn't."

"I would have done anything to protect her from that. I don't know how I could show her or tell her more how sorry I am for all the things that she went through. I don't know what I can do about it; I can't take it away."

Megan said, "The important thing is for you to acknowledge what happened. Because I had told you about it, yet your first response was that you didn't know. And it's always like that. You want to make everything look perfect. Don't confront anyone; don't take a stand. I used to starve myself and not eat anything for days, and you wouldn't even notice. You would say I was dieting."

At my request, Janet apologized tearfully for having kept Megan in her bed until she was twelve and neglecting her during her teenage years. Then I asked her whether she could help Megan financially, and she said she certainly could. In fact, she lived alone in a huge house that she had kept because she thought one day it would belong to Megan. She had financial pressures because of the house, but she agreed that she would help Megan get started in a career after she finished college and that she would at least make the down payment on a house for the young couple.

Larry was happy about Janet's promise to help. He responded to her generosity by being more giving to Megan. Their relationship improved. They moved to a better neighborhood and were happy with the move and each other.

Mother Knows Best

Every family has rules about how men and women should relate to each other. These rules are rarely discussed explicitly but are transmitted from one generation to the next. Young people watch their parents' interaction as they are growing up, then often choose a marital partner with whom they can repeat the same type of relationship they observed between their parents. Even when the marriage of the parents was very unhappy, young people seem to find someone with whom they can share the same kind of unhappiness.

It is curious that people will seek to repeat old family patterns rather than find happier relationships. Perhaps it's more important to feel secure in a relationship that is familiar than to face the uncertainty of a relationship that could be happy but may be uncomfortable in unfamiliar ways.

Larry and Megan came from similar family backgrounds. Both had strong mothers and irresponsible, broke fathers. Larry's father had abandoned the family when he was very young, so his mother was his sole support until he grew up. Megan's father barely functioned until the divorce. Then he could no longer be counted on. He became an alcoholic, didn't make any money, refused to give Megan any financial or emotional support, and even attempted to molest her. Megan's and Larry's mothers, on the other hand, were self-supporting, caring, and very involved with their children.

This is the type of family organization that I refer to as "Mother Knows Best." The father is no good, financially or emotionally. The mother works, manages the finances, and makes the decisions while the couple is still married, which is often not for long. She tends to be generous to the children and helps start them off in life with an education and career. The children stay very involved with her and often have difficulty committing to a spouse because the strongest bond is to the mother. They also have difficulty becoming independent and successful financially because they know they can always count on their mother, who will make any sacrifice to help them.

In choosing one another, Megan and Larry were setting up their family to repeat this pattern. Megan was the more intelligent, educated, and competent of the two. Larry had only a high school education, while Megan had a bachelor's degree from a prestigious college. Larry's vocation for rock and roll did not make him a strong reed to lean on. His inclination to make quick money with the least possible effort, even to the point of dancing as a male stripper, indicated a weakness of character reminiscent of his and Megan's fathers. Even in terms of their mothers, Megan was in a stronger position than Larry. Her mother was richer and more successful.

I knew I had to do everything possible to influence the young couple's relationship so that their marriage would be better than their parents', even though I could see that in choosing each other they were already starting to repeat old family patterns. I followed certain steps that are useful in having a fresh start.

Steps to Improve a Young Couple's Relationship

In the previous chapter, I described four steps that a young couple can follow to improve their marriage. Here are four more steps involving the previous generation.

Blame Your Own Parents

Don't blame yourself. Don't blame your spouse. Instead, make every effort to explain your defects, personality flaws, and interpersonal problems by blaming your parents. All behaviors that are not appreciated by your spouse can be explained as originating in your childhood. Everything that is unpleasant about you is the result of parental abuse, neglect, emotional distance, intrusiveness, or any other defects that your parents might have had or be construed to have.

This strategy exonerates you from any responsibility for your own behavior. What's more, it takes the pressure off your spouse who might otherwise feel responsible for eliciting your bad temper. By blaming your parents, you also help your spouse see you in a favorable light. Instead of thinking that you are angry, depressed, or irresponsible, your loved one will realize that you are only a victim who deserves love and compassion.

Nothing unites a couple better than to have a common enemy. Your parents can help your marriage by becoming the objects of your blame. You don't need to fear that blaming your parents will jeopardize their relationship with you. They might become temporarily upset, but it will pass. Rarely do we get that kind of unconditional love from siblings or friends. That's why it is not a good idea to blame other people like we blame our parents. Other people may not forgive us.

Money, affection, and food are three areas in which it is particularly useful to blame your parents. Whatever your defects are in these areas, you can explain them away with reference to your childhood memories. For example, if you are stingy with money, don't want to share your income with your spouse, or refuse to give presents, it's because of the way you were raised. Your father never gave you presents, or perhaps your mother was an overspender, or maybe your parents were poor. These are all good justifications for your lack of generosity.

If you are either too cold or too demanding of affection, it could be because your parents stifled you with love or never gave you enough. If you are too fat or too thin, it's because of the eating habits your parents encouraged. The list could go on. Just like there is cause and effect, the past comes before the present, and our parents are the source of our past and present difficulties.

Needless to say, the "blaming the parents" strategy is specifically appropriate for this phase of a young couple's development. As time passes and the marriage develops, it must ultimately be replaced by a more mature acceptance and understanding that takes more personal responsibility. There is no absolute truth in blaming. It is simply a useful strategy in certain life stages.

Don't Blame Your Spouse's Parents

You can usually blame your own parents without risk, but not so your spouse's parents. They love their own child, but their love for you is another matter. It is not unconditional. If you criticize or antagonize them, you run the risk of harming your relationship with them—and with your spouse—in ways that might be difficult to mend.

In the presence of your in-laws, be polite and noncommittal. But be sure to compensate your spouse for this impartiality by agreeing vehemently in private with all the criticisms that your spouse expresses with regard to your in-laws. It's best, however, not to contribute any criticisms of your own. Some people are harsh on their own parents but become upset if anyone else criticizes them. Instead, you can commiserate with comments such as "It must have been difficult for you!" "How you must have suffered!" "My parents were just like that," or "My parents were exactly the opposite."

These comments are harmless unless you begin to compete with each other as to who had the worse parents. In that case, it's usually best to concede that your spouse's parents were worse (unless yours were guilty of child abuse or another such crime). If you continuously compete for whose parents were worse or who suffered most, you run the risk of losing the positive effect of blaming parents, which could divide you instead of bringing you closer.

Ask Your Parents to Do Reparation

Tell your parents what you need. Give them the possibility of helping you. It is generally not a good idea to say that you want them to buy you a car because they never tucked you in at night or because they didn't help you with your homework. If you put it that way, you will probably only get into endless arguments about what really happened when you were a child.

Instead, it is best to just let them know how much you need them now. Be kind but firm, and don't stop pursuing them until they help you in the ways that you consider reasonable.

Forgive Your Parents

Once your parents have helped you enough, forgive them in your own heart. This act does not preclude you, in the privacy of your home, from continuing to blame them. If you need them as a common enemy, by all means continue to use them as such. Even if they know you are still doing this, they may understand because they did the same to their own parents.

However, be careful not to lose track of the fact that many years have passed since your childhood. Your parents were different people then from what they are now. You can blame the parents of your childhood while enjoying the parents of your adult life.

To blame one's parents may be age-appropriate for a young couple who are having difficulties, but this is a stage that must be overcome. Most young people need to recognize the fact that although they may sometimes need to blame their parents, this need does not necessarily reflect any truth about whether the parents are actually to blame. If a forty-five-year-old couple is still using the strategy of blaming the parents, they have not matured and are stuck at the life stage of young couples engaged in war and competition. Instead, a mature couple develops compassion, based on their own experience as parents, and can acknowledge that they are responsible for their own lives.

Eventually we grow older and have our own children. Just as money plays a secret role in our lives as young adults, so it continues to exert a hidden power in what we can do for our children. We'll consider this role in the next chapter.

Chapter Four

What Parents Can Do for Children with Money

As parents, we want to prepare our children for the world they will find outside the family. In this world is a system of rewards and punishments by which certain behaviors are compensated in specific ways. The reward may be money, power, love, or recognition. In school, children can gain recognition, power, and love, but not money. The meaning of money and how to obtain it is taught in the family.

When we give our children allowances in exchange for chores, rewards for good grades, and special presents, we help them understand how to make money. Also, when our children share our struggle to make a living and make ends meet, we teach them a lesson about the reality of material life. In our families, children learn to save, negotiate for money, work for money, be stingy, and be generous.

We can give money as a reward to increase a child's self-esteem, or we can give it to emphasize that the child has nothing and the parent has everything. That is, we can use money to elevate or patronize a child. This is one of the many secret meanings of money.

Creating Artificial Needs

Parents often give children things that create artificial needs, perhaps with the deliberate intent of dominating by taking away those needful things. For example, a father may give his son a stereo and later threaten that if the boy's grades are not good, he will take it away. If he hadn't given the stereo in the first place, perhaps the boy would have had nothing that he liked so much that he could be threatened with the possibility of its loss.

A tension develops between the person who gives, creating needs, and the person who receives and feels threatened with loss. This tension is such that it is difficult to restore good feelings. If the stereo is taken away, the boy will resent not only the loss but the fact that it was given to him in the first place, feeling that it was probably given as a manipulation. If the stereo is not taken away, the father will feel taken advantage of: he gives so much and asks for so little! Father and son will become more and more distant.

When the creation of new needs, the satisfaction of these needs, and the threat to remove the needful thing are repeated over time, father and son will communicate almost exclusively with regard to this process and will talk about little else. Money and needful things will become the commodity of the relationship.

Strings Attached

The issue is what strings are attached to giving. Some parents want their children not to suffer any deprivation. They give them everything they want, plus many things that the children don't necessarily need. They make it difficult for children to become independent or separate from the parents.

Other parents want their children to suffer deprivation, thinking that perhaps this will build their character. They give little or nothing, with the result that the children feel neglected, unloved, and unsure of themselves, and therefore they have difficulty separating from the parents. The issue for parents is how much they should give to their children—what is the right measure—how to strike a balance so that the children don't stay dependent.

The same issue exists in love relationships. The young man who falls in love with a deprived young woman naturally wants to give her things. How much should he give so that she will be happy with him instead of needing what he gives, wanting him more for the money than for himself?

Guilt Versus Generosity

One of the interesting but confusing issues about money is that sometimes there are motives to the giving of money that do not correspond to the perceptions of the receiver. Money can be given for one reason and received with a very different interpretation of why the money was given.

For instance, a mother invites her married daughter and grandchildren to a summer vacation. From the mother's point of view, she is giving a generous gift. From the daughter's point of view, the mother is attempting to interfere with her family life and her marriage. The counterpart is that the mother may give the vacation with the intent of interfering, and the daughter may interpret that the mother is simply being generous.

Sometimes parents give with generosity and sometimes with feelings of guilt. Giving with generosity is easy to understand. When a friend's birthday comes along, for example, perhaps one could give a birthday card or even just a phone call, yet one might decide to buy something special, not out of a sense of obligation but simply out of good feelings and generosity toward a friend. By contrast, a father may give an expensive birthday present to a child, not out of generosity but out of guilt feelings for having neglected the child.

In the family, money is exchanged for obligation (parents have the obligation to feed their children), generosity (love), guilt feelings, favors (such as companionship or chores), or on the basis of entitlement. Some exchanges of money are clear and not open to negotiation. Others, however, are constantly renegotiated and may form the major content of conversation in the family. For example, should parents buy a new pair of sneakers for their son because he needs them or on the basis of whether the boy regularly does the dishes? Similarly, does a parent pay for a college education as an obligation, out of generosity, out of guilt, because the young person is entitled, or in exchange for favors such as the young person's companionship and attentions?

The problem is that sometimes money is given for one reason and received with a very different interpretation. For example, a parent may pay for college in exchange for companionship and attention from the young person; but the youth may not feel obligated to any exchange, thinking that there is an entitlement to be supported through college. These differences are rarely made explicitly, and they can covertly undermine relationships for years.

The Power Base of Children

Typically in a family, parents have a financial power base in that they can give or withhold, while children need to develop a power base with some commodity other than money. Some children look to elicit guilt in the parents as a way of obtaining money. Others offer love and understanding. Some think that they can achieve power with their own accomplishments, for example, by getting good grades.

Tacit quid pro quos exist in families that are rarely made explicit and often lead to unhappiness. For example, a mother may feel that because she raised a child with love and generosity, she is entitled to the child's affection or care later in life. The child may feel that there was an obligation to being raised with love and generosity for the simple fact of being a child and that the mother deserves nothing in exchange. The child may feel no obligation to take care of the aging parent or even pay for a nursing home. That is, money can be used or demanded as a substitute for love in the quid pro quos that constantly occur in families, yet, because there are few explicit cultural rules, no one knows what is the appropriate exchange.

Children may refuse to participate in a quid pro quo by arguing, for example, that parents are really giving out of guilt and not generosity. The guilt may be for real or imaginary psychological damage. In this way, children avoid moving from the receiving end to the giving position in a family. They don't owe anything. When children learn to obtain money and privileges by eliciting guilt in the parents, they can start a career of extortion and will have difficulty separating from the parents or succeeding in life.

It's important for parents to understand that everyone occasionally feels guilty toward their children, but it's also critical not to allow the children to obtain anything through extortion. Otherwise, the children will always have to think of themselves as damaged, in order to benefit from the parents' guilt. A child who obtains small favors from eliciting guilt in the parents may grow up to be an adult supported by the parents on a permanent basis because of the damage the parents feel they did.

What Is and Is Not Negotiable

Many families don't make explicit what is negotiable and what is not negotiable. Children are constantly threatened with losing what they are given, because parents don't clarify what is given as an obligation and what is given as part of an exchange. The children, then, don't differentiate between what is and is not negotiable, nor do they learn to understand on what conditions things are given or withheld.

Let's say a boy turns sixteen and is given the use of the family car. He thinks he is entitled to it because of his age and because he helps to drive the younger siblings around. Yet, when he gets a bad grade, the parents refuse to let him use the car. The boy feels that the car belongs to the family and therefore to him. The parents feel that the use of the car is a privilege to be constantly negotiated. The boy cannot understand which of the family possessions belong to him. The parents talk about "our house," "our car," "our things," but it isn't clear to the son that any of this really belongs to him. The confusion is even more evident when parents threaten to expel a child from the house. How can he be expelled from his own house? The message to the child is that he can sometimes have the use of "our house," "our car," "our television," "our phone," but he is basically destitute—none of this belongs to him. He only has the use of these things if he achieves the goals the parents set for him, but these goals are constantly changing.

Parents need to be clear with the children and with each other about these issues:

- What belongs to everyone in the family, and therefore cannot be withheld as punishment
- What belongs only to the parents but can be used by the children if they follow certain rules or achieve certain goals
- What belongs to each child and cannot be taken away or used to reward or punish

Parents may decide, for example, that the TV belongs to them and can be used as a reward or a punishment, but the teddy bear belongs to the child and cannot be taken away. The child needs to know ahead of time that it is the TV and not the teddy bear that can be taken away and under what circumstances it might be taken away. In order to have a secure reality, the child needs to know what consequences to expect. Failing in school may mean no TV, but it doesn't mean expulsion from the family.

We want our children to be at least as clear about what are the consequences of misbehavior as we are. We know that if we park in a no parking space, we might get a ticket, but we are certain that we won't get the death penalty.

As children grow up and become spouses, the confusion as to what consequences to expect for certain behaviors can become even greater. Each spouse comes from a family with an implicit quid pro quo, and usually the rules of exchange are different for each family of origin. Each spouse expects the other to relate to the in-laws according to the implicit quid pro quo of their own family, and each has difficulty in understanding and accepting the implicit rules of the other family.

Mythical Family Accounting

Very few of us enjoy bookkeeping or accounting. Those who do can spend long hours reading the books of a corporation. The accounting of a company is its history. Going through the entries, we can understand the creation of the company, the relationship of the partners, and the bonds with clients and providers. Accounting laws are universal.

Families also have an accounting system. In contrast to corporations, however, every family has its own method of accounting. What's more, each family member also has a special accounting system that is different from that of every other member. So each one has a different idea of what is fair with regard to money. Parents will give money to their children as payment for chores, as compensation for guilt, as reward for good grades. But children often misunderstand why parents give money. Siblings keep an accounting of what each and every other sibling receives and demand fairness according to each one's own accounting system.

Another difference between a family and a corporation is that in a business, the books are closed at the end of a fiscal year and a balance is made. There is often a specific day, at an annual meeting, when this balance is officially discussed. A statute of limitations states that the balance cannot be contested after a certain period of time. In the family, however, there is no annual balance, no specific day for discussion, and no statute of limitations. Therefore, money issues in the family don't have a past and a present. They are never closed; nothing is final. Money issues are always in the present, to be rehashed over and over again. They are passed from one generation to the next. Problems and complaints are inherited. In addition, instead of having one set of accounting books in the family, there is one set of books per family member. These books are usually contradictory with one another.

For example, Beth had not spoken to her sister, Joanne, for many years. They had quarreled over what to do with the modest family home when their father died ten years ago. Years later, the home had gone up in value, and Beth wanted to sell it. She asked Amy, her youngest daughter, to speak to Joanne about selling the house. Joanne said to Amy that she would only agree to the sale if Beth returned the ring that Joanne had given her when their mother died, twenty years ago, long before their father's death. Amy had never heard about this ring. Joanne explained that it was their mother's wedding ring, and she had consented to giving it to Beth because she had wanted so much to have it. But now Joanne was angry at Beth because of the disagreement about the family home, and she wanted the ring back.

When Amy told Beth that Joanne wanted the ring back, Beth said that she no longer had it. She had given it to her cousin on the occasion of her marriage. Joanne expected that, in order to negotiate the sale of the house, she would renegotiate with Beth the present of the ring, when the ring didn't even belong to Beth any more. Joanne and Beth had different systems of accounting, and there was no statute of limitations, no balance that was final.

In a corporation, the books exist in reality. In the family, the books are imaginary. They only exist in the minds of the different family members. Rarely does a person actually keep a written account of the money transactions in the family. Since memory is unreliable, it is impossible to determine which transactions really took place over the years. The accounting methods are idiosyncratic and mythical to each family member. But to understand money in the family, we have to realize that this confusing method of accounting is a reality.

Yet, certain helpful steps can be taken:

1. All family members need to be aware of the rules by which money is distributed. When parents give money to children, it has to be very clear whether it is for obedience, respect, love, good grades, or entitlement.

2. A family can set aside one day each year to go over the finances, so that everyone understands who got what money and why. Discussion is welcome and complaints can be heard on this day, but not at other times. Parents and children, at this meeting, must share an understanding of the economic priorities in the family, how the family got to the point where they are now, and what are the plans for the future.

3. The hierarchy must be clarified so that everyone understands who decides how the money will be distributed.

4. There needs to be a statute of limitations, so that after a certain number of years, accounts are closed and cannot be revised.

The goal is to have one accounting system that everyone understands, so that who gave what to whom for what is clear to everyone, and so that accounts can be closed, instead of having resentments and reproaches go on for years.

Entitlement and Extortion

Most of us try to be fair and give equally to all our children. We believe that it's important to love all our children, and we express that love through giving not only affection but also material things. Obviously, it's important to give equally to our children when they are young. Otherwise we create bad feeling, low self-esteem, envy, and hatred. Curiously, when our children become adults, most of us still continue to feel that we should love them and give to them equally. Yet some of our children are nicer to us than others; they have different needs, different problems. How to be fair is a constant dilemma for parents. Should we give according to what we receive from the children? Should we give according to each child's needs and problems?

When the children feel that we haven't been fair, they sometimes turn to extortion. Andrea came to see me because she wanted to reconcile with her parents, to whom she hadn't talked for several years.

"I have certain problems in my life," she said with great anxiety, "that lead me to believe that my father abused me sexually when I was a child. I don't have any memories of abuse, yet I suspect that he did, so I'm angry and I haven't talked to my parents in years. At this point, I would like to reconcile with them. I want you to help me to remember whether I was abused or not."

We talked about her childhood and went over all her memories, as I tried to help her remember, but after a couple of hours with no results, I told her, "Look, the best way to find out if you were abused is to talk to your parents, put your concerns out in the open, and we can see what they say. Let me call your parents and invite them to come to one session."

She agreed. When I called the parents, they said they would be happy to drive the long distance from another state to see Andrea. They didn't know why she wouldn't speak with them. They had only one daughter, and they wanted very much to have a relationship with her.

When the parents walked in, I looked at the older couple and doubted that this father would have committed sexual abuse. Yet I know from experience that one cannot trust first impressions, so I was careful to keep an open mind. Anything was possible. I encouraged Andrea to open up to her parents and tell them her concerns, but she couldn't do it. She said she had old resentments, felt her childhood had been sad, was unhappy, but couldn't bring up the subject of the sexual abuse. The parents said that she had been a happy child and were surprised and puzzled.

"Andrea," I said after about half an hour of this type of conversation, "go to the waiting room and I will explain, in private, your concerns to your parents. In this way, you won't be embarrassed, and then I can bring you in and we can all discuss the situation together."

Andrea left, and I explained to the parents that, even though she couldn't remember, she thought that she had been sexually abused by her father.

"You may have made bad mistakes as parents in the past," I said, "but this is your opportunity to make up for some of those mistakes. It's very important for Andrea's mental health that she know the truth. You can see how anxious and upset she is. She has to know what happened to her as a child."

The parents were appalled, shocked, bewildered. Both assured me there was no sexual abuse, no abuse of any kind. The father was deeply hurt by the accusation. I decided to call Andrea back into the room.

"We have reached an impasse," I said. "You think you were sexually molested, and your parents say there was no such thing. I think that what is important is to move on so that you can have a relationship with your parents again. And I think that, whether or not there was sexual abuse, your father must have done something very bad to you that you have this idea that he sexually molested you as a child. Maybe what he did was not sexual abuse, but it must have been something that hurt you very much. So I think he needs to do reparation. Andrea, I want you to think about what your father can do to make some kind of reparation, even if it's only symbolic, because, of course there is nothing that can really compensate for hurting a child."

Andrea flew into a rage. She screamed and raved that there was no reparation possible, that she was insulted at the mere idea, that what her father had done was horrible. I insisted and waited for her to calm down. After a while she dried her tears.

"I want $50,000," she said, to the surprise of everyone in the room.

The father was furious. "This is extortion, blackmail," he said, turning red in the face. "I will give her nothing."

I began to negotiate for Andrea. As we talked, I understood that Andrea was angry because when her brother graduated from college, the father had given him $50,000 to open a business.

"You gave it to him . . . . ."
"Not to me . . ."
— "Poor me"

When Andrea graduated from college, he had given her nothing because she was a girl. That was why she wanted $50,000. In Andrea's own particular method of accounting, she preferred to think that the parents owed her because of abuse than because they had favored her brother.

I asked Andrea what she planned to do with the money. "I want to go to graduate school and get a Ph.D. in psychology," she said.

The father absolutely refused to give her the money, but I got him to compromise. He promised that he would pay for her tuition and all her living expenses for as long as it took to get her Ph.D. This was a very good deal for Andrea, since obviously the expense would be much higher than $50,000.

Parents and daughter left my office arm in arm, cheerfully talking about where they would have dinner together. This was the most extravagant way I've heard of getting paid for one's graduate school tuition.

How to Give to Your Children

You can give to your children in ways that will help them grow, or you can give in ways that will do more harm than good. Here are some guidelines to consider when giving to your children.

Be Careful About What Needs You Create

It is inevitable that parents create needs in children. Every time a parent makes a gift to a child, the parent is creating a need. For example, if the gift is a Barbie doll and the parent spends time playing with the child and doll, a need is probably developed in the child to want to play with Barbie dolls in the future. In addition, the danger is always there of endless upgrading. One Barbie leads to the desire for several Barbies, besides Barbie furniture, Barbie clothes, and a Barbie swimming pool, to name a few.

There is a continuity between children's toys and adult toys. The gift of a bike, for example, may lead to the desire for a faster, more expensive model as the child grows up. When a parent makes a gift, it can have long-term consequences. Consequently, a parent must think carefully about what needs to create. It's particularly important to consider whether the gift is the expression of the parent's own frustrated desires. For example, a father may give an adult son a dirt bike because it's what *he* would have liked to drive and not necessarily what the son wants. Yet, receiving the gift of the dirt bike may create a whole new series of needs in the son.   *Gifts?*

Don't Give to Take Away

Because of the control that parents have over their children, it is always possible for parents to give gifts that they can later take back. If a child doesn't do well in school or if the chores are not done, for example, the child might be punished by losing the gifts that were received for a birthday. If an adolescent comes home late, he may be prohibited from using the family car the next day. Gifts and privileges are often used in negotiations about obligations. Yet if a parent continuously gives to take away, the child might become frustrated and despondent to the point where revenge for the frustrations become the overriding concern in the young person's life.

Don't Punish While Giving

A gift can be accompanied by kind, loving words or by threats and insults. When a gift is associated with aggression and put-downs, a conflict is created that may kill all ambition in a young person. To take a son to a football game, for example, is a privilege and gift, but if the opportunity is used to put down the child in public, then the punishment is double because the put-downs happen in a situation that should have been particularly happy. Be careful only to reward when you are rewarding and only to punish when you are punishing.

Don't Use Money to Teach Lessons

Interestingly, 81 percent of the population feels that they don't know how to handle their own money well, yet almost 100 percent of parents say that they use money to teach lessons to their children. I am not referring here to simple lessons such as using money as a reward for work well done or payment for chores. Almost everyone uses money in this way. What I am talking about is a subtle, twisted lesson that is confusing in its ambiguity.

For example, a father offered to buy a car for his young married son. He said he was willing to spend $1,000. The son found a car that was in mint condition and had been reduced from $1,400 to $1,200. With great effort he convinced the seller to lower the price even more down to $1,100, but the seller said that was absolutely the final price. The son happily reported to his father that he had found a great car for $1,100. But the father said he'd teach him a lesson. He had said $1,000, and he would stick exactly to it, not one dollar more. The son went back to the seller, having put together all his savings, and gave him $100, asking him to keep it a secret and make the price $1,000 to satisfy the father.

At settlement, the father said, "See, you got the car and I taught you a lesson!" What was the lesson? What the son learned was to lie, cheat, and bribe. This is the kind of lesson it's better not to teach.

Avoid Creating Resentment

All the previous circumstances—creating artificial needs, giving in order to take, punishing while giving, and using money to teach lessons—create resentments in children that are very difficult to overcome. Sometimes parents are inclined to create resentments because the resentful person is always dependent on the object of the resentment. That is, a resentful child is a dependent child. When parents have difficulty in letting their children grow, they create resentments that will keep children immature and prevent them from getting on with their lives.

When aware of this issue, a parent can exercise self-control and avoid a dependence that makes everyone unhappy. When resentment comes associated with gifts, children demand more and more gifts, hoping to elicit in the parent the resentment that the child has suffered. But the more gifts the child gets, the more dependent the relationship, and the more resentful the child.

Don't Let Your Children Use Impoverishment as Power

Some parents put themselves in the situation in which children want to teach them a lesson about money. Some children want to make their parents pay forever. One way to do this is to become impoverished. The parents then can always worry about the child, feeling badly if they support the child and guilty if they don't. Impoverishment is a source of power over those that care. If we don't have anything, not only can't we give but also we're always on the receiving end.

Be Fair

Distribute money equitably among your children. If you give more to one than to the others, be very clear with them about why. Express explicitly to the children what they have to do in order to obtain money from you. Don't let yourself be blackmailed, but if you make mistakes and favor a child unfairly, do reparation to the others. When you do reparation, be explicit about what the reparation is for. If you don't talk openly about money, even when you are fair, your children won't know it. Your children need to understand your idea of what is fair in relation to money. Otherwise they will never understand when you are fair.

As our children grow older, they take so much of our attention that we sometimes don't realize how our relationship with our spouse is changing. In the next chapter, we will look at what can happen in a marriage as time goes by.

Chapter Five

Money and the Middle Years

As soon as a child is conceived, a couple has become a triad, an institution, a family. The relationship between the spouses must change. The sibling-type competitiveness that characterized the relationship of the young couple must give way to cooperation. But this cooperation is not always easy. Partners often take secret actions with respect to money, which have consequences that can be better understood and remedied once we realize their hidden meaning.

When the couple becomes a triad, special issues arise about how to plan income and expenses in the future. After children, the couple has become an institution with all the administrative problems of a bureaucracy. When the couple becomes a family, it develops problems similar to those of any corporation. They have entered a pyramidal structure with executives at the top and underlings at the bottom. In this chapter, we will look at the different types of behavior that the partners can present, what actions they can take with respect to money, and the consequences of these actions on each other and on the family.

The particular way in which a business is run depends on the personal preferences of the partners. Miserliness, competitiveness, resentment, hostility, and betrayal are common problems between partners. The relationship that the business will have with other businesses and the community also depends on the preferences of the partners. Some businesses want to be exactly like their competition; others want to be totally different. Some businesses want to be first, and some are content with being second. After reading this chapter, you will realize that the organizational behavior of the family is very similar to that of any business enterprise.

This chapter deals with the middle years of marriage—roughly between the birth of the first child and fifteen to twenty years of marriage. The couple has to decide who is going to make what money and how it will be spent. These decisions are influenced by the secret meaning that money and material possessions have for each spouse. At this time, the issue of how much to give and how much one is entitled to receive becomes most crucial, and conflicts of loyalty become most intense. We will look at the impact of the children, different kinds of financial styles among couples, crises like affairs, deprivation and loss, unhappiness at work, and the problems of success.

Financial Impact of Children

With the birth of the first child, the relationship of the couple becomes more and more complementary and less and less symmetrical.

A young couple typically has a symmetrical relationship: the man and woman are equal; both work or study; both have similar needs and equal say in the decisions. As the wife progresses into the first pregnancy, the relationship becomes more and more complementary. She is pregnant; he is not. This is a big, very noticeable difference. She needs special support, her body is compromised, her needs change, and she depends more on him.

The transition into the middle years of marriage is difficult. Husband and wife have different needs, and they need each other in a different way. Whereas before each looked to the other to satisfy their narcissistic needs and complement what was lacking in each one's personality, now they need each other in very practical ways. They have to provide for and raise a child together. Conflicts of loyalty and jealousy become very intense or appear in the relationship for the first time. Does the wife prefer the child to the husband? Is she jealous about the husband's love for the child? Is he jealous because she loves the child more than she loves him?

New decisions must be made. Will the wife stay home with the child, or will the husband? Will she go back to work? When? What will happen if the couple loses the income she brings in? Is staying home a sacrifice or privilege? These are difficult choices, and it is at this time that many couples establish the patterns of how to deal with each other around money issues.

For example, a young woman asked for a consultation about a marital problem. She said, however, that her husband refused to come to see me so she would have to come alone. Nancy was very attractive, although so thin that she made a curious contrast with the plump toddler she carried. She said that she was trapped in a terrible marriage with no affection, no communication, and no way out.

She was an attorney who had met her husband, Gary, when they were both in law school. When they graduated, they decided to get married, so both found jobs in the same city. The plan was that she would work until she got pregnant and then she would stay home until the youngest child was going to school. Gary would continue to work and provide for the family. So Nancy worked until the end of the first pregnancy and then stayed home.

As soon as the first child was born, Gary began to complain about having to work while she stayed home and enjoyed the baby. He became demanding and resentful of the relationship between mother and child and tried to spend as much time as possible with the baby, ignoring the wife.

When Nancy became pregnant with the second child, his resentment grew. He worked long hours in a cut-throat environment and hated what he did. Nancy offered that she could go back to work and he could stay home with the children. He refused, saying that now he had advanced so much that he was several years ahead of the wife in income potential so she could never make as much as he was bringing home. Until then, he had given her his paycheck, but now he began to make more money and withhold it from her. He complained about her spending and kept cutting her funds to the point that, in order to feed the children, she was living on rice and beans. He refused to talk to her or have sex with her and threatened that if she left him, he would win custody of the two children because he was a much better lawyer.

With difficulty I convinced Nancy to let me speak with her parents. I asked them to come to town to meet with me and discuss their daughter's difficult marital situation, which they were quite aware of. I told them that Nancy was being emotionally abused by her husband, who took advantage of his superior professional and financial situation.

"I don't think it was a good idea for Nancy to give up her career as a lawyer," I said. "I suspect that she lost her husband's respect, and he has been taking advantage of her vulnerability now that she depends on him. I want you to help her get back into her career, become financially independent, and then I think her husband will treat her once again as an equal."

"How can we do that?" asked the father.

"We don't like to interfere in their marriage," added the mother.

"All I need from you," I said, "is a little financial help for Nancy. I want you to loan her enough money so she can hire a very good nanny to take care of the children while she goes back to work. I would like her to find a law firm where, even if she doesn't make much money to begin with, she can learn and eventually excel."

"I agree," said the father. "She needs to get back into her career."

"Once she's working," I continued, "I think her husband will be interested in her again. If he's not, I suspect the marriage won't last much longer, but then she will be prepared to support herself."

Nancy found the nanny and went back to work. Gary had a few tantrums about how she was neglecting the children. Soon, however, he found that he had new respect for his wife. He became sexually interested in her, and they became a couple again.

Guilty Fathers

Some husbands feel guilty because they can go on with their careers unencumbered with concerns about the child. They may then feel that they can never bring home enough money to compensate for the sacrifices the wife makes by staying home. In this type of marriage, the wife tends to make all the decisions about how money should be spent, while the husband works hard at making money.

Sometimes the father's guilt extends to the children. Later in life, the father may be subject to extortion by adult children who realize that they can easily exploit him on the basis of his guilty feelings over the alleged neglect to which he subjected them during their childhood.

Jerry, a well-known head of a government institute, entered my office with tears in his eyes.

"It's all my fault," he said. "I have had the good luck in life to have a fascinating career that has totally absorbed me. So, over the years, I have neglected my children. I know that I am responsible for all their problems."

His children were, in fact, quite successful in their various careers. Three out of five had professional degrees, and the other two were working toward them. Yet, most of the children were constantly asking the father for financial support.

After talking with the mother and children about how much the father had really participated in the family's life over the years, I concluded that he had not been more neglectful than most men who have to support five children. But perhaps the children had felt that even when the father was with them, his mind was on the very important international issues that he had to deal with in his job.

One of Jerry's daughters was now "depressed." At one point in the therapy the "depressed" daughter advised her sister on how to get the father's attention by pretending to be mentally ill. Both daughters resented that Jerry was gone so often that he could not attend many therapy sessions, even though he was giving them the financial help they demanded.

Although Jerry's wife of thirty years assured me that he had been a good father, it took tremendous effort on my part to convince Jerry that he was being taken advantage of by his children and had no reason to feel guilty. As soon as he was convinced, however, he made it very clear that he would not put up with any more extortion. Instantly, the children seemed to become more mature and, demanding less of their father, began to take better care of their own lives, and his daughter announced that she was out of her "depression."

Resentful Wives

Some wives are resentful because they feel coerced to stay home with the children, when they would rather be working or pursuing their careers. They feel imposed upon by the husband and jealous because he has an adult life outside the home while also enjoying the love of the child. They feel they deserve more out of life and tend to make the husband pay, literally insisting on having control of the money and demanding the right to have a say about how much money the husband should bring home.

For example, an old employee of my father once approached me about how to solve a difficult marital problem. He said that his wife charged him to have sexual relationships. Tom explained that not only did he give her his whole paycheck, but he had to find moonlighting jobs to be able to pay her every time they had sex. He explained that his wife, Sue, felt that she deserved this compensation because she had to stay home all day. She had given a monetary value to every exchange with the husband, including sex.

I told him that he had to make drastic changes in the relationship. Every evening he should spend at least half an hour talking to his wife. Instead of paying her to have sex, he should pay her and then just be affectionate with her, holding her and kissing her but without having sex.

"She's going to ask why are you acting so strangely," I said. "And you're going to tell her that love is more important than sex. If you do this for a few weeks, I guarantee that she will stop charging you for sex."

When Tom started to give love to his wife, she responded in kind and began to initiate sex without charging.

Guilty Mothers

Other wives feel it is a privilege to stay home and feel guilty about the fact that the husband has to work. They tend to become submissive and involved with the children at the cost of their relationship with the husband. They tend to exclude him from getting involved himself with the children. They tend not to get involved with the husband's work. They don't handle the money but complain that they don't know anything about the family money. They often feel that the husband is a tyrant.

Alex, for example, complained that he could never enjoy sex with his wife because she was always listening to the intercom to make sure her two babies were breathing properly. During intercourse she would suddenly imagine that she could no longer hear their breathing and would rush to the nursery to make sure that they were alright.

"You don't love the children like I do," Dora would explain to Alex. Yet every time that Alex tried to play with the children, Dora complained that he was too rough.

When Alex tried to talk about money with Dora or about his problems with his father in relation to the family business, she would answer, "It's too complicated for me—you can just decide yourself."

Dora was an excellent cook and was always waiting on Alex. Yet when she talked with her friends, she would say that he was a tyrant who didn't let her participate in financial decisions, neglected the children, and demanded to be waited on hand and foot.

With the help of a therapist, Dora realized that she had become submissive because of her guilt feelings about Alex's difficult work and complicated relationships with his family. She began to understand the submissiveness that she herself had arranged to compensate for her guilt feelings. Consequently, she began to help Alex with his work and participate in his family life.

Financial Styles Among Couples

Couples need to make decisions about lifestyle. These decisions are directly tied to money and to how much debt the couple will accumulate. The amount of debt, in turn, will determine how much they have to work. Lifestyle and decisions about money will determine what kind of a relationship the spouses will have.

Few couples actually sit down to discuss lifestyle and make rational decisions. Most people float from one choice to the next, not giving too much thought to how decisions should be made. We tend to imitate the lifestyle choices of our friends and family, even though we may not approve of these choices.

Besides selecting lifestyle and incurring debt, married couples have to deal with problems of competitiveness, loyalty, distance and closeness, old family money, and the crises that they will inevitably face in the course of the marriage.

The Competitive Couple

Some couples never make the transition from the competitive relationship of their early years to a complementary relationship as parents to their children. They behave more like brother and sister than like husband and wife. They continue to struggle with each other as if they were equal, attempting to share all responsibilities and competing with each other about who is more successful. They tend to refuse to share the money that they make and keep money in separate bank accounts. They believe that each one has the right over their own money and refuse to share. They seem to lose the sense that marriage is a collaborative relationship.

Doug and Diane, for example, were very different, mainly because Doug was fifteen years older than Diane. Yet they had much in common because they were both therapists and writers. Also, the age difference between them was compensated because Doug was the youngest of four siblings while Diane was the oldest of three. Doug knew how to relate to an older sister, and Diane knew how to relate to a younger brother.

They applied this experience to the marriage and collaborated with the competitiveness of brother and sister. They had separate bank accounts; over ten years of marriage they didn't put their money in a common pool. They directed a therapy institute but refused to discuss any thoughts about therapy, for fear that one would steal the other's ideas or publish them first. Each time one published a book, the other would carefully screen the manuscript for any stolen ideas. They were stingy and suspicious with each other not only about money but also about their thoughts, which made it difficult for them to communicate about anything interesting.

Doug and Diane could live like this for ten years because they were successful and affluent. But then the economic recession of the 1990s hit them hard. For their institute to survive, they had to take money from their separate bank accounts and put it in a common pool. As they began to face their creditors, their most trusted employee left them and opened a competing business. Doug and Diane had to face loss and betrayal together. They were sharing the same struggle for survival, and they finally became a couple, sharing instead of competing.

The Emotionally Distant Couple

When a couple chooses to have complementary roles—for example, she takes care of the children while he works—they can become more extreme and more set in these roles over time. The wife may refuse to talk about anything except the home and the children. The husband may be totally absorbed by his work. Over the years the spouses will find that they have less and less in common with each other. They will fight less about money, but they will become distant and uninvolved. When they change to a different arrangement—for example, as the children grow older, the wife goes back to work—they may begin to fight again about money in the way they used to do when they were a young couple without children.

Competitiveness leads to war, but relationships that are totally complementary lead to boredom and distance. A minimum struggle over some issues must exist for the couple to have something in common.

In our time, relationships can become particularly distant when the spouses each have their own money, work, friends, and family relationships. Edda was a dancer who worked late hours and dined with her friends at dawn. Claude got up at five in the morning to study the behavior of the stock market, spending the rest of the morning at his computer. At night he would go to sleep at precisely the time when she was leaving for the theater. They would only meet at six in the evening for a few minutes while she was dressing for work and at five in the morning when she would come home. They had separate rooms because of their different schedules, no children, separate bank accounts, and different friends. They were comfortable in a stable, unsatisfactory relationship.

Eventually Claude decided he needed a vacation, bought a boat in the Caribbean, and invited Edda to spend a month on the boat with him. Together for the first time, in the middle of the sea, they found that they had to talk. Edda wouldn't stop talking about money: what she was entitled to, what properties should be in her name, what she would get if he died, how to have financial security. After two weeks on the boat, they separated permanently.

Sometimes it is precisely the separate lifestyles that keep a couple together. Different lifestyles can lead to the illusion that they are distant, not because they are very incompatible but because they have different schedules and social contexts. When pushed into a situation of closeness, they may realize that they disagree about everything and eventually separate. Money issues didn't separate Edda and Claude when they were not talking. But as soon as they talked about money, they realized that they didn't have a common plan.

A particularly difficult conflict emerges in cases in which the wife has put the husband through school by working and then expects him to pay her back, either by giving her money or doing the same for her. He may refuse to do it or even take the opportunity to leave her, believing that he doesn't owe her anything.

Marcia was a nurse who put her husband Juan through medical school by working long hours in a hospital. Juan came from a poor Puerto Rican family. He was Catholic, so they had five children, one right after the other. When Juan finished medical school, he wanted specialized training to become a surgeon. Marcia continued to work so he could finish his training. As soon as he began to make money as a surgeon, he fell in love with a friend of Marcia's, who was also a nurse but ten years younger. They divorced, Marcia never recovered the money that she had invested in his career, and he pays minimum child support.

Conflicts of Loyalty

In the middle years, couples are often plagued by conflicts of loyalty. And decisions about money are always intertwined with these conflicts. As our children are growing, our parents are aging and they need us more. This is also the time when we are most focused on our careers. Many dilemmas arise. Should one be loyal to one's parents above all? Or should the first priority be to our work, our career? Choices are difficult because work and career are the future, our security, where the money comes from to support the family. But what about the children—aren't they our greatest love? They are the ones we really want to help. How to be loyal to their interests while still supporting the family, staying married to their mother or father, and not betraying our parents—this is the dilemma most of us face.

Brenda, a patient of mine, fell in love and married for the second time. Her husband, Steve, was the only son of a widowed mother. A few years after the marriage, Steve's mother became seriously ill. Steve began to help her financially and spend most of his time with her. Brenda complained that he was spending too much time with his mother and giving her too much money.

"You have to choose between your wife and your mother," Brenda said to Steve.

"If you make me choose, I'll have to choose my mother," replied Steve. "She is old, sick, and alone. I can't abandon her."

Brenda left with her two children from a previous marriage. Without Steve's help, she found it was difficult to make ends meet, and she had to work hard, couldn't support her children, and gave her son to her own mother to raise. She became lonely and depressed and eventually attempted suicide.

Asking a man to choose between his wife and his mother is generally not a good idea. There are other ways to solve the conflict of loyalty without having to make such drastic choices.

Another typical conflict of loyalty is between one's children and the family business. In family-owned businesses, parents usually encourage children to work in the family company. When the children are incompetent, the parents can be torn in conflicts of loyalty between what is best for the children and what is best for the company.

The Weinsteins came to see me because they were extremely concerned about their youngest daughter, Julie. She was a thirty-five-year-old MBA who, after working successfully for a big firm, had been fired for deceitful behavior. She had become depressed and confined herself to her apartment, where she spent all her time listening to John Bradshaw audiotapes. She had become more and more withdrawn, and the parents thought that she was behaving like someone who had been inducted into a cult.

"There's something wrong with all our children," said Julie's mother. "Julie is the youngest of six, three boys and three girls, all in their forties. None of them have married, and only Julie has left home."

I thought that this was unusual and asked how the other children were doing. The father, who bore an extraordinary resemblance to my own immigrant grandfather, explained, "I have to tell you, Doctor, I have had to make a difficult decision in my life. I own a big, very successful business that I struggled with for my entire life. All the children, except Julie, worked for the business, and, because of them, the company was failing. Their incompetence was making me sick. One day I got up, went to the factory, and fired them all. I think I made the right decision. I had to choose between my children and my company, and I chose the company because that is our livelihood."

"How did the children respond?" I asked.

"Not very well," said the father. "Some don't talk to me; others are cold. None of them are doing well. They are all struggling."

It had been a strange coincidence that Julie was fired from her job at approximately the same time as her siblings were fired from theirs. Also, at the same time as her father worried about his children, she became concerned with her inner child. He was torn in the conflict between the children and the company. She was torn in the conflict between her adult self and her child self. As long as her father refused to incorporate her siblings back into the company, she would refuse to integrate her inner child with her adult life, and she would remain withdrawn and brainwashed.

I convinced the father that he had to help each of his adult children succeed in life. He talked with each one, gave them loans, offered advice, and set each one up in their own business. As Julie watched her siblings improve, she returned to her adult life, reconnecting with work and friends.

Old Family Money

Marital problems are particularly difficult when one of the spouses has old family money. The issue is, Who does the old family money belong to? Isn't it meant just to be passed from one generation to the next, without ever being spent? Isn't it supposed to give security to many generations to come? Even worse, the issue arises, Am I loved for myself or for my money?

When there is enough old family money that the couple doesn't have to work, life can become meaningless. One or both spouses may suffer, questioning themselves as to whether they could have succeeded in life if they had had to work. These self-doubts can undermine a person's character and have a negative effect on the marriage.

The worst problem arising from old family money is that it encourages a couple to live beyond their means. Charlie and Jane consulted me about terrible marital fights. Charlie had been married previously and lived extravagantly with his first wife, without saving any money. Charlie had expected to inherit a fortune from his father. When they divorced, his wife didn't get anything because they hadn't made any money or bought any property during the marriage. After he married Jane, the second wife, his father died. Now he felt he had to share the inheritance with his first wife, because they had lived together for fifteen years under the agreement that they didn't need to work or save because they were going to inherit. Jane objected, which was the cause of the terrible fights.

Charlie had made an explicit agreement with his first wife, which he was willing to respect even after divorcing. Most couples, however, make tacit agreements that they don't feel obligated to after the divorce. I congratulated Jane on having chosen a husband who had such a strong sense of "noblesse oblige" and convinced her to let Charlie share some of his inheritance with his first wife. I suggested that Charlie take a part of his inheritance and divide it equally between his first wife and Jane. Consequently, both his conscience and Jane were satisfied.

When one of the spouses has old family money, the couple tends to live according to the situation of the wealthier one. The idea is that the old family money is something that both have the right to enjoy. The use of the money, however, is different from its ownership. The sad surprise comes during divorce, when the less wealthy spouse discovers that she or he has no claim to the other's old family money.

Addiction to Spending

Sometimes during the middle years, one of the spouses may become addicted to spending. The wife, for example, may run up large bills on credit cards for clothes or items that she buys for the home and children. Or the husband may purchase a sports car, boat, expensive stereo system, and so on. Each of the spouses will feel guilty about their spending but will not be able to do anything to stop it. Usually this kind of spending reflects a lack of agreement and joint planning about what are the priorities in the couple's life. Sometimes the addiction reflects low self-esteem on the part of the spender. At other times the spending is a form of revenge for not feeling loved or appreciated.

Reckless spending is one of the most detrimental factors that undermines the stability of a marriage. It is well known that disagreements about money are a leading cause of divorce. Most probably these disagreements have to do with reckless spending on the part of one of the spouses.

Ilene and Jeffrey had been married for three years when they consulted me because Jeffrey was considering ending the marriage. He said that Ilene's reckless spending was ruining him and destroying their relationship. I listened to how Ilene would run up a credit card only to obtain a new credit card that she would quickly charge up to the limit. Both spouses had good jobs and shared their income but were quite different in terms of spending money. Jeffrey believed in saving and never using credit cards. Ilene did not disagree with him, yet she couldn't stop buying. She felt everything she bought was necessary or important. Clothes, kitchen utensils, furniture, presents for relatives were among the many necessities that Ilene couldn't refrain from purchasing. She had promised that she would not spend more than what she made, but she couldn't keep that promise, and Jeffrey repeatedly had to save her from angry creditors.

I sympathized with Jeffrey's problem, Ilene's wish to change, and her difficulty in doing so. I said that Jeffrey would have to help her in an unusual way. Every time that Ilene bought something, except for groceries, Jeffrey would buy something twice as expensive and totally useless. He would continue to do so—even if it meant that their apartment would be full of unnecessary objects—until both spouses agreed that Ilene's spending was no longer a problem. Jeffrey put this plan into effect, and, in a few weeks, Ilene became very careful about money. She was now the one that worried about how to pay for the credit cards Jeffrey was running up, and she hated the things that he brought home.

The Miser and the Spender

After addiction to spending, probably miserliness is the greatest cause of marital unhappiness, particularly in the traditional marriage. When a couple has an agreement that one is the provider and the other is the homemaker, sometimes the provider insists on having a greater say on how money should be spent. When the provider refuses to spend on what the homemaker needs or wants, the homemaker perceives the spouse as a miser, deliberately depriving the family of the things they need. The nonproviding spouse will often take revenge, sometimes using the children or the in-laws for this purpose. The couple will have difficulty in rising above the grim drudgery of everyday life, not taking risks, perhaps gaining security, but at the sacrifice of their happiness.

Even in marriages in which both spouses are providers, frequently one is a miser and the other is a spender. The more miserly one becomes, the more the other may tend to spend to protest or to compensate for the miserliness. The more the spender spends, the more the miser will refuse to do the same or to participate in the spending of the other spouse. Husband and wife will drift apart, with many recriminations and few projects in common. This combination usually leads to divorce.

A special situation is when someone is a spender with themselves and a miser with others. For example, Alfred was very wealthy. He lived with a young woman who didn't have any money of her own. Frequently he made long trips for pleasure or business. He had an agreement with his girlfriend by which he would always travel first class and she would travel in coach. He would give her the money for the difference in price between the coach and the first-class ticket, and she could spend that money shopping. He refused to give her any money for shopping if she didn't fly in coach. Alfred didn't hesitate to spend on himself but was stingy with his girlfriend, not an uncommon arrangement.

Another special situation involves people who are stingy with themselves and generous with others. Carl owned only three pairs of pants, because as he said, "One I have on, one is in the closet, and one is at the cleaners." Yet his wife's closet was full of the expensive clothes that he bought for her, always thinking that she didn't have enough. This type of arrangement can make the wife so happy that the marriage will last a long time.

Deprivation

Most young couples enter marriage with the enthusiasm of people going on a camping vacation: "It will have its uncomfortable moments," they think, "but mostly, it will be fun." It's an unpleasant surprise to discover that they have more needs and wants than they thought they had and that there is never enough money.

This fact becomes most evident in the middle years of marriage. The husband may resent that the wife is not eager to get a better job, and the wife may be disappointed that the husband is not a better provider. The couple often find themselves spending more than they make and accusing each other of mismanaging the money. Arguments about money can become the daily conversation of the couple.

Conflicts about deprivation can arise even when the couple is extremely wealthy. A couple of small means suddenly hit the jackpot when the husband, whose hobby was to write horror novels, became a best-selling author. He began to publish one best-seller after another, and the wife took charge of managing the money. Their obligations grew; there were charities that depended on them; they had developed an organization that they had to maintain. The wife began to demand that the husband publish one best-seller per year. She said it was the only way of maintaining their standard of living. The husband accused the wife of not even knowing how much money they had or where it was. They found themselves arguing as bitterly about their wealth as they had argued about their deprivation when they were younger.

Keeping Up with the Joneses

During the middle years of marriage, many couples find themselves trapped in an economic situation they didn't deliberately choose. Few couples sit down to plan what they truly want to do with their money. Decisions are made, one by one, based on what others are doing, not necessarily what is best for their particular situation.

For example, the couple may buy a house with a mortgage that is a little too much for them to carry. They may purchase two cars that are more luxurious than what they really need. They may find that they have spent too much on decoration and furniture or family vacations. Most of these purchases are made only because others make them; it is what is expected. Material possessions provide a sense of belonging to a certain social group whose members all live in similar houses and own similar things. Many couples seem to be held together by the common goal of accumulating material possessions.

The Pretense of Power

Couples have to negotiate who is going to have power over what in the marriage. Some couples simply divide areas of responsibility. In a traditional marriage, the wife, for example, may be responsible for the home and children and make all the decisions about how money should be spent in these areas. The husband may be responsible for making the money and deciding how to invest it. In this type of marriage, conflict usually develops when the husband wants to invest money that the wife would prefer to spend on the family.

In other couples, a tacit agreement emerges that the one who makes more money has more power and therefore can make all the decisions on how money should be spent or, at least, can veto the decisions made by the other spouse. The spouse who doesn't work or who makes less money tends to become secretive and resentful of the power of the other spouse. Sometimes the one with less power will seek to develop a power base by making a coalition with the children against the other spouse. The one who makes the most money then feels excluded from the family and resentful of the bond between the other family members.

In some couples, one of the spouses pretends to have power over the money and the other accepts this pretense. The make-believe may be to appease a difficult spouse, satisfy a parent, or benefit the children.

"I've been living a lie all my life," said Dorothy with tears in her eyes. "I've been so unfair to my father! All my life I thought he was a bum who never worked. I believed that my mother supported the family, and it was the other way around."

Dorothy's parents, Leo and Rachel, were poor immigrants who started a family business in a storefront under their apartment. Rachel managed the store while Leo found customers for the export business and manufacturers to produce the goods. He was always out negotiating, while Rachel was in the store. Rachel constantly complained about how hard she worked while the husband didn't do anything. The children grew up believing that the father didn't work, not only because of Rachel's complaints but also because Leo was always out, so they didn't see him working. They thought that the mother supported the family because she was the one that they saw handling the money at the cash register. Since she gave the children money, without the father's knowledge, they thought that the money was hers. Later in life when the children had their own businesses, they realized that their father had been working very hard all along, with little appreciation from the family.

Crises

The middle years of marriage are sometimes characterized by going from one crisis to another. One seems to be on an obstacle course, where as soon as one hurdle is overcome, another looms bigger.

Crises arise around the children: problems with school, social difficulties, illness. There are crises with the grandparents: they are growing older; perhaps they are sick and the younger couple has to take care of them. The death of the parents is probably the most serious of these crises. Crises at work can come up: change of job, difficulties, loss of job, too much debt. Loss of job or change of job are serious crises that can also jeopardize the stability of the family.

Many of these crises involve issues of money. For example, a child's problem may be solved by paying for a private school. Yet the parents may not agree that this is the best way to spend their money and may fight bitterly over this issue. Perhaps the struggle is that even though they agree on the private school, they cannot find the money to pay for it. Perhaps at this point they fight over whether the wife should go to work or whether they should use the family savings. The same can happen around illness or elderly parents. The issue is where to get the money and how to spend it.

Affairs

In the middle years of marriage a couple can often reach a balance in their sexuality. As the husband's sexual desire decreases with age, the wife's increases until they are about balanced. Unfortunately, this is often for only a short period of time.

Two typical crises develop. One is that the wife's sexual drive continues to increase while his decreases. So eventually she might find sexual satisfaction with another man. The second typical crisis is the Lolita complex. The man feels his sexual drive is diminishing because his wife is not attractive enough and looks for a younger woman, thinking that she will revive his sexuality. Sometimes she does, but then he has to begin the whole cycle again and start the creation of a new family.

Some couples never survive the first affair of one of the spouses. The other spouse, hurt in his or her pride, will end the marriage. Sometimes the spouse who is having the affair is humiliated when the affair is discovered and ends the marriage out of shame.

Sometimes there may be several affairs during the middle years of the marriage and yet the marriage will continue. It may be that the affairs themselves are what stabilizes the marriage.

A particularly difficult situation is when money is involved in the affairs. A husband may be supporting another woman or even another family. A wife may fall into the hands of an unscrupulous man who extorts money from her. When affairs are tied to financial loss or to deception about money, the marriage almost inevitably ends with a separation.

Fear of Loss

In uncertain economic times, the fear of losing one's job or savings is always there. These anxieties can cause quarrels over money and often cause many problems, such as physical illness, depression, and sexual difficulties. The fear of loss may become the single most important motivator for one or both spouses. The relationship of each one to their work will then take priority over the relationship with each other or with the children. This situation can go on for years and take all the joy out of the marriage.

Fear of loss is particularly prevalent among those who grew up in poverty, or during a depression, or whose lives were tied to the social circumstances of emigration and war. A special kind of anxiety is suffered by those who fell into poverty coming from a secure economic position and were able to rise again into financial security. They are plagued by the fear that they may lose everything again. This fear will keep people working forever at jobs that they hate. It can turn into greed and separate family members as they fight over who has more.[1]

Sarah and Aaron suffered great persecution before they emigrated to the United States and then poverty during their first few years as immigrants. Their five children always lived in fear of financial loss. They didn't pursue their vocation, feeling that financial security was a more important goal. The competition between the children escalated, from an early age, to the point of hatred. One of them, Michael, systematically robbed the others for no particular reason, since he didn't need the money. The need was psychological; he needed the security that money gave him. His wife struggled with severe attacks of panic. Michael's daughter, Martine, consulted me about her troubled adolescent son. He said to me, "Grandpa told me how he stole from the family." The boy couldn't understand it—he had been raised in financial stability. To help him with his depression, I arranged for his mother, Martine, to tell him as much of the truth as she knew about her father and to do reparation to the rest of the family for what her father had stolen.

It is difficult for those who were raised with security to understand the exaggerated anxiety about money of the children of immigrants. Often that generation is more driven and suffers more than its own parents from the fear of loss.

Most of the middle class also suffer from financial insecurity and the fear of loss because there is no guarantee that they'll be able to stay in their social class. People born into a wealthy family usually feel secure, believing that the money will be there forever. The poor and the working class usually feel they are in a stable situation. They were born into a way of life, and it's improbable that their financial situation will improve or deteriorate greatly. In contrast, those born into the middle class have no guarantee that they'll stay there. They need to study hard, work even harder, and it's only through great effort that they are able to stay in the social class into which they were born.

Often the children of middle-class parents, looking at their effort, reject it, not just because it seems mindless but because it isn't even pleasurable. So middle-class couples, fearful of loss, are pulled apart because they work so hard and are saddened because their children usually don't even appreciate their effort.

Unhappiness at Work

It is common knowledge how easy it is to bring work problems home. When a person is unhappy at work, he or she tends to take out the frustrations on the spouse or children, with the expected unhappy results. Sometimes the depression that results from unhappiness at work leads to feelings of pessimism about the marriage and family. At other times, spouses who are unhappy will feel that they deserve more from the family because they are so unhappy at work. Unfortunately, life is not like that, and one does not usually get compensated within the family for the misery suffered outside.

= compensation! =

Eventually, the feelings associated with difficulties at work can be transmitted to the children, who will also suffer from low self-esteem.

In some situations, unhappiness at work is used as a manipulation with the family. My mother used to say, "Don't disturb your father. Be careful what you say—he has many problems at work." Whenever one of us needed something, had a problem, or wanted to make some plans, Mother insisted that the conversation had to be postponed because Father was too preoccupied with work problems. Father's unhappiness at work protected him from having to deal with his children and empowered my mother to be the intermediary in our relationship with him.

Success

During the middle years of marriage, one of the spouses may become successful at work, rich, or famous. Success is almost as difficult to handle as failure. The successful spouse may become more demanding or distant, and the couple may not be able to overcome the fact that one is much more successful than the other. With success often comes arrogance and pride, which are characteristics not conducive to the best relationships.

Even more complicated, the successful spouse may alternate between arrogance and fear. It is common for highly successful people to feel that they are impostors who could be discovered any minute. They may live in anguish, feeling that they do not deserve their success, that their personality is just a facade, and that they cannot live up to their accomplishments. Consequently, they demand constant support and reassurance, with its inevitable toll on the marriage.

Boredom

Economic stability often leads to boredom. Without a struggle to make ends meet, ennui can become an all-pervasive problem in the middle years of marriage. The spouse is like an old shoe; conversations and behaviors become totally predictable; there is no excitement, no sense of adventure. Fortunately, most couples are distracted from their boredom by the many crises that occur during these years. But in periods of calm, the boredom tends to set in.

To counter the boredom, some spouses will embark on activities that are not what they truly desire, such as going on shopping sprees, traveling, having more children, and fighting over everything. Together with the boredom may come the feeling that surely there must be someone out there who is more interesting, more exciting, less boring. As a consequence, infidelity can become a problem. Sometimes, the drive to make money or the urge to spend it will replace the affair as a solace from the boredom of the marriage.

Death of a Parent

For most people the death of a parent is the most traumatic event in their lives, and it often happens during the middle years of marriage, adding stress to the relationship. It is difficult to be happy with one's spouse when one is mourning the death of a parent.

More stress is added when there is a will and inheritance. No matter how carefully planned, the will is one thing from the point of view of its author and a very different thing from the perspective of the heirs. Most wills elicit bad feelings and conflicts, as the heirs argue about who was really entitled, who deserves a gift, and who should be compensated for what. The battle around the will typically interferes with the happiness of the marriage.

Roger and Betty came to see me because of a sexual problem. After four years of marriage, Roger had lost interest in sex. He didn't have erections, or he lost them, or he suffered from premature ejaculation. Betty blamed herself, thinking that it had all started because she had become more demanding sexually of Roger. I asked them about their families, lives, and projects, and I discovered that Roger had lost his father and shortly after—two years ago—his mother. He and Betty had spent the last two years fighting with the family over the mother's will. She had left the family home to Roger's sister and had virtually disinherited Roger. His sexual difficulties dated exactly from the time when the mother's will had been read to him. Although he had managed to reach a satisfactory agreement with his sister about the inheritance, he hadn't been able to recover sexually. Yet Roger and Betty had never connected the two events: the will and Roger's sexual difficulties.

I said that if it had been his mother's intention to make him feel castrated, she had certainly succeeded. He had not thought of it that way. After a few weeks of sex therapy, he recovered and resumed a happy sex life with Betty.

How to Survive the Middle Years

You can do certain things to increase the chances that your marriage will last through the middle years. Let's take a look at some of them.

Insist on Handling Money Issues Together

Even though it is tempting to delegate all unpleasant money matters to your spouse, don't give in to this temptation. To avoid resentments and confrontations, it is best to negotiate money issues one by one and together. Plan to have business meetings regularly to discuss these matters. It is particularly important to make joint decisions about how money will be spent on the children.[2]

Make Time-Limited Decisions

"But you agreed." "Remember what you said." "It was your decision." Most of us hear these remarks as accusations repeated over and over again. Remember that very few decisions are for life, and set a time frame on your agreements. You can decide where to live and what car to drive, but the decisions can be valid only for a limited time. Things change, you and your spouse change, financial conditions are different, and everything can be renegotiated.

Renegotiate If You Feel Guilty or Resentful

Decisions about work or money can breed guilt and resentment, which, if unheeded, can fester and ruin your marriage. If you are experiencing feelings of guilt or resentment or if you suspect that your spouse is suffering from these feelings, sit down to renegotiate. Negotiations should end in a satisfactory way for both. A marriage is not good if one wins and one loses.

Don't Renegotiate Forever

Some couples spend their whole life in a struggle of bargaining and negotiating with each other. Set a time limit on how many times you can renegotiate an issue until the decision becomes final. In this way you can have time to move to other things.

Give More Than You Take

Refuse to be competitive. Try always to give more than you take. Remember that love always comes together with generosity. Don't keep count of how much each gives to the other. Marriage is a quid pro quo in which the exchanges take place over many years, and each spouse is eventually on the receiving end. What you are giving today in money, you will probably get back in love, security, sex, and vice versa.

Don't Be Distant

Don't expect your spouse to realize that you're unhappy about money because you have become distant. If you are unhappy, say so overtly. Don't let money problems interfere with your intimacy or ability to enjoy good times with your spouse. Be sympathetic to the other's anxieties about money and work, be sincere about your own difficulties, but remember that you can't let money troubles interfere with your marriage.

It's Better to Work Than Not to Work

You are the only one who really knows if you should work or not. If you're not sure, it's better to work. If you have to work more because of the family's financial needs, don't hesitate to do so. If you don't really need to work for the money, you probably will be better off anyway if you work. Don't work only if it is not financially necessary and you feel your work will be detrimental to the family.

Avoid Affairs

It is difficult to predict the financial consequences of affairs. Among the many negative consequences are blackmail, the loss of financial leverage in cases of divorce, the possibility of children from an extramarital union, and the possibility of having to support a lover or a lover's family.

Be a Miser/Be a Spender

If you are a reckless spender, practice miserliness. If you are a miser, once in a while you must practice reckless spending. A miser is usually married to a reckless spender. By taking on your spouse's typical behavior, you will be showing understanding and empathy, and you will be appreciated. It's good once in a while to put yourself in the other's shoes.

Accept That There Is Never Enough Money

Instead of being surprised every time you have financial difficulties, accept the fact that this is the natural order of things. Money difficulties are a fact of life, and if you accept them as such, you will not suffer as much anguish. Knowing that there is never enough money will help you in avoiding the "keeping up with the Joneses" syndrome, because you will be able to accept that you can never keep up. To worry constantly about money is similar to worrying constantly about death. We all know we have to die, yet thinking about it all the time is not conducive to happiness.

Use Money to Avoid Boredom

If you have to choose between boredom in your marriage and over-spending, choose overspending. Many marriages are saved by a vacation that was taken even though it couldn't be afforded. Similarly, a timely present can make a big difference in winning a spouse's affection.

Ask Yourself Whether Money Is Really the Issue

Money per se is never the issue. The issue is whether money represents needful things or interpersonal relationships. When money represents needful things, we argue about material possessions, such as who owns a house, how much of an inheritance we are entitled to, how much can we spend. When money represents interpersonal relations, a financial conflict may not be about money but rather about secret or hidden issues of control, power, caring, appreciation, commitment, or sex.

If you are not successful in negotiating the middle years of marriage, you will probably go through divorce and remarriage. So pay attention to the next chapter.

Chapter Six

Divorce and the Second Marriage

Divorce is such a brutal process, the scars it leaves are so deep and so lasting, that it influences all our love relationships for the rest of our life. That's why the emotional and economic ties to our second spouse will be marked by the process of divorce that precedes our second marriage.

We often feel we really only know our husband or wife after the divorce. No matter how long the first marriage, no matter how well we thought we knew our spouse, during the divorce we must come to terms with the fact that the person whom we had chosen to be with for our whole life, the father or mother of our children, feels like a stranger. The unsavory personality that emerges in our spouse during the divorce shocks and surprises us. Is this the person we used to know so well? How could she or he have changed so much?

There are two possible explanations. One is that each spouse actually suffers a personality change during the process of divorce. Another is that we turn our spouse into a stranger because we don't love him or her any more. Yet, since we are hardly aware of this process, we have trouble coping with the changes we observe. We need our spouse to become a stranger in order to divorce, but we are hurt and angry when our spouse has become this alien person. After the divorce, we'll never trust our judgment about another person as we did before.

Divorce and the Loss of Innocence

Divorce is the killing of a marriage. Three kinds of bonds can be destroyed: the bond between the spouses, the bond of money and material possessions, and the bond of love for the children. In cases where the couple was involved in a family business, the bond to the business is also usually destroyed.

Ideally, we would like to break only the first bond—the bond between the spouses. But in order to accomplish this, we need to turn our spouse into a stranger, so the other bonds also suffer. It's difficult to share our children and material possessions with a stranger. During the divorce, one or both spouses may be suspicious about the motivations of the other, about their intentions with regard to money or the children. The more estranged we become from our spouse, the more we think, Why should this stranger have my children or money?

The most savage battles during divorce are often fought about money, but perhaps the most painful ones are about the children. The most painful situation is when one of the parents rejects the children, abandoning or neglecting them as if the divorce were from the children also, not just from the spouse. The intent is to hurt the other parent, and this hurt is usually greater than the pain of lost money.

Consequences of Divorce

After going through the divorce process, we are never the same. Just like the soldier coming home from the war, some of us suffer drastic changes in our personality or outlook toward life.

Ron came to see me because he was depressed. He had married for the first time in his mid thirties, after becoming quite success-ful in his career as hotel manager. His wife, Cheryl, was ten years younger. She had been his assistant at work.

The marriage began with problems when Ron had given her herpes. Cheryl was repulsed and lost interest in sex. Yet they had planned to have children right away, so they did, and Cheryl stayed home to take care of them. They had a traditional marriage. Ron continued his habit of being a workaholic, and Cheryl devoted her-self to the home and children. They rarely had sex, seldom talked, and didn't have anything in common.

Cheryl was unhappy with this arrangement, particularly because she felt that Ron was not involved enough with the children. She nagged him constantly to spend more time with them but he would not change. Ron and Cheryl had a stable, unsatisfactory marriage.

Then Ron lost his job when the hotel industry began to suffer from the recession of the 1990s. The shock was unexpected, and Ron couldn't find another job. He was now spending all his time at home, and the unsatisfactory aspects of the marriage became more apparent. Cheryl took the children, moved into her parent's house in another city, and sued for divorce.

Ron became more depressed. "I began to obsess about the mistakes I had made during the marriage," he told me with tears in his eyes. "I was a bad husband and a bad father. Now that I don't have the children, I realize how important they are to me and how important I am to them."

"Are you working now? Are you supporting them?" I asked.

"Not really," he answered. "I could get a job as hotel manager, but it would have to be in some other city, and I don't want to be far from the children. I realize now that money isn't important; what's important is the relationship with my children. So, in answer to your question, I'm selling soap from door to door and making just a little money, enough to support myself. That's why Cheryl and the children are living with my in-laws."

"You're selling soap!" I said, surprised because I knew that he had been a successful executive. "Surely you could be doing something better than that!"

"But I don't want to," he muttered. "I'm glad I'm not a workaholic any more. This way I can spend all the time I want with the children."

"And your father-in-law is going to support them?" I asked.

"Cheryl is going back to school, and maybe she'll get a job," he answered.

I looked at him with disbelief. "In just a few years, when your children are seventeen, eighteen years old and they're getting ready to go to college," I projected him into the future, "you won't have any money to pay for their education. Are you going to explain that you don't have money because you didn't want to work so you could spend more time with them?"

"I didn't think of it that way," he replied.

"I wonder what your children are thinking now about their successful executive father going from door to door selling soap!" After a pause, I asked, "What kind of example are you giving them?"

"You think that maybe it's not a good example?" he seemed puzzled.

"I think you're completely crazy." I wanted to shock him back to reality. "For thousands of years parents have been expected to support their children. There must be some wisdom to that! And all of a sudden you stop working and decide that it's better to just play with them instead. Do you realize that soon they'll grow to be young men and you'll have to explain your decision?"

"What do you think I should do?" He appeared even more confused than before.

"I think you should look for a job in your industry," I answered. "Since it's important to be close to your children, try to get a job nearby, but take whatever you can. Just be sure to insist, as part of your contract, that the company will pay for several trips a year to visit your children."

There was a long pause.

"And start supporting them and saving for their college education," I added.

There was another long pause. Then he said, "I think you're right. I must have been temporarily insane." He thanked me and left.

A year later he called to thank me again. He had been lucky enough to get a job in town and was very happy with his decision to continue to provide for his children.

"When I came to see you," he said, "I had lost track of who I was and what I wanted. You brought me back to reality."

Cheryl couldn't change Ron during their marriage. But eventually the trauma of divorce changed him into what Cheryl wanted him to be. At first he thought he had become a sensitive, caring father, but in fact, he had become an insecure, irresponsible play-mate of the children. I had reminded him of what he had forgot-ten: that his obligation as a father was not only to spend time playing with them but also to provide and plan for their future.

Lost Illusions

Together with divorce comes a loss of innocence. We realize that marriage is not for life. If we remarry, we want to protect ourselves and our children from the consequences of a new divorce. So we enter the second marriage already thinking about divorce. We real-ize the importance of preparing for the worst.

The main conflict for the person entering a second marriage is between the desire to be in love and the fear of being ultimately disappointed. The fear may be not only that the second marriage will end like the first but also that you will only really know what the second spouse is like after the second divorce.

After a divorce, you typically fall in love with someone whom you think is the opposite of the first spouse. Even so, you are often so afraid of repeating the first relationship that during the second marriage, you constantly look for clues that the second spouse might be like the first one.

One of the curious paradoxes of the second marriage is that as time goes by, the second spouse seems to become more and more like the first spouse. You soon realize, with great shock, that you married the same person all over again.

There is a simple explanation, however. *You* are the same per-son. The second spouse is interacting with you, and therefore the range of behaviors is limited by the way you act. His or her per-sonality is only one side of the interaction, so, no matter who is your spouse, each one will appear to behave similarly.

Unfortunately, since you are who you are and the second spouse seems to you like the first, you fear that the end of the second mar-riage will be like the end of the first marriage. So you begin to plan the end of the second marriage from its very beginning. You want a better marriage. But how can a marriage last when you are already planning its demise?

One difference between the first and second marriage is that the first marriage may end in a few days of unpleasant discussions about money at the divorce settlement, while the second marriage may consist of spreading those unpleasant discussions from the beginning. In the first marriage, money is an issue at the end; in the second marriage, because you have lost your innocence, money is often an issue from the very beginning and all through the marriage.

Choosing the Second Spouse

Most of us learn from our experience and are more careful in the choice of our second spouse. We are more mature, we know ourselves better (or at least we think we do), and we look for someone with whom we can be truly compatible. Yet, the experience of the first marriage and the subsequent divorce influences our choice of the second spouse in complex ways.

Typically, we look for someone who is totally different from the first spouse, so we look for opposite traits. For example, if the first spouse was stingy, we look for a spender. If the first spouse was lazy, we look for a workaholic. The problem is that relationships are complementary: where there is a spender, there has to be a miser; where there is a workaholic, there has to be a sloth. So you may find that you are no longer married to a miser—you have become the miser. you are no longer married to the sloth—you have become the sloth.

Marriage can consist of a permanent struggle to change the other, to make the spouse more like yourself. So you find yourself trying to change the spender, whom you so carefully picked, into the miser that you have now become.

To complicate things further, during the first marriage, each spouse thinks that the other has the best role. One spouse will say, for example, "What movie shall we see?" or "What restaurant shall we go to?" and the other will answer, "I don't know, you choose."

Since one of the spouses refuses to choose, the other always has to make the decisions. The one who always makes the decisions thinks that the other is happier and struggles to trade roles. The one who never decides thinks that the other spouse has a better time and also struggles to trade roles.

In the second marriage, each spouse is quick to grab the opposite role of what they had in the first marriage. This is the chance, for example, for the one who always made the decisions to be able to say, "I don't know, you decide." Soon, however, each is disappointed with their part. The spouse who is now the undecided one gets tired of eating in bad restaurants and watching bad movies. A certain nostalgia develops for the first spouse, the one who just went along and didn't make any decisions. The second marriage can also be seen as the struggle of two people trying to trade roles.

What We Bring to the Second Marriage

When entering a second marriage, how do we deal with mortgages, health insurance, debt, education for our children, taxes, and retirement? Entering a new marriage is entering a new economic enterprise. We carry the financial obligations to our first families, and we want to maintain some financial independence since we now understand that a second divorce is possible.

In the first marriage, there are common goals, children belong to both spouses, properties are in both names, and money goes into one pot. Spouses talk about "we" and "ours," and each is part of one nuclear family that consists of parents and children. No matter how a couple tries to re-create this situation in a second marriage, it is seldom the same.

In the second marriage, the family unit may consist of parents and children, plus children from previous marriages, plus the spouse's children from other unions, plus ex-spouses. The goals are not just the goals of the marriage. There are goals carried over from the previous relationship.

We are often in conflict between the commitment to children of a first union and the commitment to the second spouse. Sometimes we don't even allow our second spouse to have a say in our decisions with respect to our money or children. The exception is when there were no children of the first marriage; then the primary commitment is to the second marriage.

The institution of the second marriage is fairly new in the world, dating from the time when laws were passed permitting divorce and remarriage. In the past, second and third marriages were the result of the death of a spouse, and the difficulties in commitment arising from widowhood are quite different from those of divorce. Hopefully we will be able to develop customs, rules of etiquette, and rituals for how to deal with divorce and remarriage. But few of these exist now. Most of us fumble around in a morass of confusion as to what is the right way to proceed.

No matter how poor or wealthy a person is, the emotional ties to the first marriage or the products of the first marriage (children, business, property) become a source of financial (and emotional) stress in the second marriage.

Most of us enter our first marriage quite innocently, with few financial assets and willing to share everything. We learn the hard way and, in the second marriage, are much less willing to share our material worldly possessions, having understood the solace they can provide from the hardships of emotional deprivation. If we are slow learners, our parents and children from first marriages won't hesitate to warn us about the ravages of emotional entanglements that will lead us from our true commitment. Concomitantly with these warnings, our new spouse may advise us to remember the unhappy victimization of our previous relationship. What to do?

Prenuptial Agreements

In a good business deal, a common arrangement is for one partner to have the capital and the other to have the know-how or provide the work. If the business is successful, after a certain time, the partner with the know-how will have made money, and the partner with the capital will have acquired know-how. Each partner will have become enriched by what the other provided to the relationship. On the other hand, if, after a period of time, the partner with the know-how still doesn't have any money, the business partnership is obviously not satisfactory.

A marriage is similar to a business partnership in that each spouse is supposed to be enriched by the relationship. A special problem arises in second marriages when logic dictates that the partners should make a prenuptial agreement. One or both partners have been divorced and know the importance of making clear agreements about money before the marriage, since they realize that the second marriage may also end in divorce. Yet the prenuptial agreement, by definition, precludes the enrichment of one of the partners. This type of agreement may be statistically rare, but the problems it expresses often exist in the unwritten and unnegotiated assumptions of many second marriages.

Typically, the prenuptial agreement is made because one of the spouses has more money than the other. The agreement is designed to make it impossible for the less wealthy spouse to make money from the marriage. In contrast to a business deal, a prenuptial agreement is usually designed to prevent the enrichment of one of the spouses. During the marriage, the spouse with less money will benefit from the lifestyle of the wealthier spouse. However, the prenuptial agreement guarantees that, if the marriage ends, that lifestyle ends for the less wealthy partner. This type of contract makes growth impossible.

Yet prenuptial agreements do not have to be detrimental. It all depends on the people involved. Sometimes the prenuptial agreement is signed with mistrust, but later, perhaps because the prenuptial agreement exists, the spouses are able to trust each other and become more generous.

Lindsay asked for a consultation for what she called a premarital problem. She had had a bad first marriage, was the mother of a young boy, and was now about to marry a wealthy man.

"Our relationship is very good," she said, "so I was shocked when he told me that before the wedding, I had to sign a prenuptial agreement. I guess it has to do with the fact that he has already been married three times and has to pay a lot of child support and alimony. But why does he want to marry me if he doesn't trust me? Why should I want to marry him if I have to sign a paper that says that I'll never have anything? I don't think that's the way to start a marriage."

"Are you asking my opinion?" I said. Lindsay's tone was so final that I was wondering whether she was actually consulting me or her mind was already made up.

"I want your opinion, of course," she answered.

"Your husband probably wants you to go to an attorney's office to sign the prenuptial agreement, right?" I asked.

"Right," she said.

"I think you have to go. The lawyer will say that he wants you to read the agreement, and then he will explain it to you. You have to say that you don't need to read it. If your fiancé, the man you love, wants you to sign, you will sign it without reading it because you have total trust in him."

"Why would I do that?" asked Lindsay. "What do I gain by that?"

"Trust me," I said. "If you don't sign the agreement, he still can ensure that you won't get anything, and he probably will because he won't trust you. If you sign without even reading it, he will be overwhelmed by your love, and I bet that he will respond in kind."

Lindsay signed the agreement as I had suggested, and a few days later, her fiancé purchased an enormous property and put it in her son's name. I had advised Lindsay to sign the agreement without reading it, not because I thought that she should be submissive but because I knew that, in this way, she would have the greatest financial gain.

Marrying for Money

Often people hope to marry someone who is rich and generous. They tend to deny the fact that, even though there might be a great deal of money, they can suffer deprivation. Also, they deny that money doesn't last forever and can easily be lost. Marrying for money doesn't ensure that they will ever get the money.

Lola was a beautiful woman, around fifty years old. One could guess that she had been a fashionable model even though, as she walked into my office, her mouth was drawn and her eyes were red, as if from crying.

"I'm terribly depressed. My husband recently died. I don't know if you can help me."

"You miss him," I said sympathetically.

"No," she answered. "I don't miss him at all. He was unfaithful to me, made me lose everything, and I only found out after he died!"

Little by little I was able to piece together what had happened to Lola. She was so agitated that it took some time to understand the sequence of events. Lola had been Christian's lover for twenty years and had been married to him for the last five years. Before meeting Lola, Christian, a Clark Gable look-alike, was married to another woman thirty years his senior. He had met her as a youth when he worked as a teller in a bank. He used to help her when she came to her security box and was impressed by her jewelry. She confided to him that she had been one of the wives of an Indian maharaja, and, upon the death of her husband, left India with her jewelry collection and the wisdom of her Yogi teachers. Christian saw an opportunity.

As a bank teller, Christian was able to see the wealthy widow's passport one day and realized that she was much older than she looked. He skillfully seduced her, promising always to be her devoted caretaker, and proposed marriage, knowing that he would outlive her by many years.

"When I met him," said Lola, "they had already been married for ten years. He told me she was very old, and in a short time she would die, and we would be married. What he didn't realize was that she had devoted her life to the yogi techniques of longevity, taught to her by the maharaja's teachers. To make a long story short, when she finally died, Christian was sixty-five and had chronic back pain and a bad liver. We married. Five years later he died. I expected to inherit the money he had inherited from the old lady. Suddenly, an illegitimate daughter appeared, contested the will, and got everything. She was the child of the old lady's cook. The old lady had been sleeping with the cook all along." Lola dried her tears, looked at me in the eyes, and said, "Do you think you can help me? Do I have reason to be depressed?"

Christian had married the old lady for money. Lola, in turn, had married Christian for money, when he was old and sick. Christian was cheated because the old lady lived forever. Lola was cheated because after Christian's death she lost everything. Both had lost their youth waiting for money that came too late or not at all.

The Emotional Economy of Divorce and Remarriage

The economy of the first marriage has more to do with needful things than with money per se. Young couples fight more about objects and lifestyle than about money. In contrast, the secret emotional economy of divorce and remarriage always has a great deal to do with money. The young couple, in the first marriage, talks endlessly about how to make money. In the second marriage, the conversation is sometimes equally endless about who does the money belong to and how are they going to spend it.

Maria and Roberto argued about money even before they were married. Maria's first husband had died in surgery owing to a medical error, leaving her with two children. She won a malpractice suit and was paid $1 million, which she invested conservatively in trust funds in the names of her children. She bought a beautiful house but continued to work as a translator in the court system. There, she met Roberto, who was also a translator.

Roberto was divorced and had three children from a previous marriage. He could hardly make ends meet with his salary of $28,000 a year. He paid child support and was very close to his children, always trying to meet their needs. He lived with his parents because he couldn't afford to have his own apartment.

Maria and Roberto fell in love. They had been together for three years when they came to consult me. There had been problems about money from the very beginning of the relationship. Maria wanted Roberto to be stronger and more successful than she was. She wanted him to make more money.

"I worry that if he's not stronger than me, I'll fall out of love with him," she told me, while glancing at Roberto flirtatiously out of the corner of her eye. "We Latin women like a man to be stronger than we are," she added.

Looking at the couple, I could tell that there was good chemistry between them and also a solid friendship. I hoped I would be able to help them to stay together.

"What can I do!" Roberto threw up his arms. "I like my work and I do a good job. I take every possible moonlighting job that I can get! She knows that translators don't make much money. When I say to her, 'Let's open a business together,' she says I'm just with her for her money. She doesn't want me to live with her, and she doesn't want to get married."

"We can't get married until we solve the money problem," complained Maria. "Every couple of weeks, right before his paycheck, he's broke, and he's asking me for money. He needs money for lunch or for transportation. He just can't get organized."

"What happens is that the children always need something unexpected," said Roberto "That's why I run out of money. Why can't she give me a few dollars without making a big deal? It means nothing to her with all the money she has."

Roberto and Maria's problem seems unusual because of the disparity between their incomes. Maria was making around $80,000 a year from her investments, while Roberto made only $28,000. Yet the problem is typical of couples in second marriages. How much should be set aside for the children? How to pool their resources in a fair way? Typically, in a second marriage, one spouse makes considerably more money than the other. What is fair?

Most couples solve this problem by having "yours, mine, and ours" accounts. Each has a separate bank account for their own and their children's expenses; and each deposits a certain amount of money in a joint account for the couple's living expenses, plus entertainment and travel. The issue is how to determine how much each should put into the common pot. This is not an easy decision because there can be a big difference between the spouses' incomes. If one is making $80,000 a year and the other $40,000, and they decide that each should put $12,000 in the common pot, this amount represents 15 percent of one income and 30 percent of the other.

A better arrangement is to decide that each will put in a percentage of their income, instead of a fixed amount of money. So if they decide on 20 percent each, for example, then the one making $80,000 will contribute $16,000, while the one making $40,000 will put in $8,000. This is the arrangement that I recommended to Roberto and Maria.

"Since you work together and are together most of the time," I explained, "you can have a common pot of money for daily expenses, such as lunch and transportation. You could agree that each will put in a percentage of their yearly income, let's say 5 percent, and each is entitled to use half of the money in that common pot each month for daily expenses. So Roberto will contribute $1,400 a year and Maria, $4,000 a year, and each will be entitled to spend $2,700 a year from this common pot." I anticipated Maria's objections, saying, "It's true, Maria, that there would be a little subsidy there for Roberto, but I think it's only fair because you make so much more than he does. We can start it as an experiment and see how it works out."

Another issue also had to be addressed: lifestyle. "The problem for you is that you have to decide whether you are going to bring Roberto up to the lifestyle that you are accustomed to," I said, "whether you are going to bring yourself down to his lifestyle, or what the middle point will be. I think you need to find a middle point."

I also explained to Maria that she should find strengths to admire in Roberto, other than his money-making ability. She was hopelessly ahead of him in this area—not by her own merit, not even because she had family money, but simply because of an accident of fate. It wasn't fair to expect Roberto to make as much money as she made because of her husband's tragic death. They liked my advice but continued to see me once in a while, every time that Maria felt that Roberto was taking advantage of her. With my encouragement, Maria was able to admire Roberto's excellent qualities as a father.

Maria and Roberto are unusual in that Maria has more money, while typically it's the man who has the bigger income. Yet, the problems of negotiating money are the same as in more traditional couples.

How to Make the Best of a Bad Situation

We can do certain things to increase our chances of happiness, but first, let's look more closely at divorce.

Accept That You Have to Lose

Divorce is a lose-lose situation. Everyone loses. You need to accept that you have to lose. You will find that it's easier to cope if you accept from the start that you will come out of a divorce a loser. The issue then is how you can lose in the areas where you can afford to lose, instead of losing where it is most painful. You might be able to lose money, instead of losing the children. You may lose the house, but not your savings. There are difficult choices to make, and they are best made not in the context of winning but in the context of what you prefer to lose.

Now let's discuss how to make the best of a bad situation.

Be Prepared to Give

Just as you are prepared to lose, you must be prepared to give. There will be some things that you will have to give up. It's better to think from the start about what you are willing to offer, instead of waiting to see what the other person can take away from you. This is especially so when you have children. When children are involved, you must know that you have to give a great deal. You will never be able to break off completely from your ex-spouse. The relationship through the children will continue and if your ex-spouse is deprived, the children will also be deprived.

Help the Other Save Face

A good negotiation cannot take place when one party feels humiliated. You must help your ex-spouse save face so that negotiations can be conducted. If the other party feels humiliated, he or she will strike back in anger, and you will end up losing more than you anticipated. This is particularly so when children are involved. If you don't help the other save face, the chances are that the children will be hurt.

Make Every Effort to Maintain a Bond as Parents and Friends

When children are involved, you will always have some kind of relationship with your ex-spouse. Try to make it the best possible relationship, not only to avoid hurting the children but to make life easier for yourself. It's painful to relate constantly to someone with hatred.

Don't Punish Your Ex-Spouse by Hurting the Children

You would only be hurting yourself. Some parents provoke the children to fail as a way of getting back at the ex-spouse. It's as if they were saying, "See, if you hadn't left, Johnny would not be failing in school." Avoid setting up your children to do badly as a way of getting even with your ex-spouse. Children deserve more love and attention than any ex-spouse.

A Fresh Start for the Second Marriage

Divorce is a bridge to a second marriage. If you divorce well, you decrease the excess baggage you are carrying and increase the chances that your second marriage will be a good one. Here is some specific advice for the second marriage.

Don't Turn Your Dream into a Complaint

Everyone enters a second marriage with a dream: finally, you will be with someone who is truly affectionate, sex will be wonderful, you will take wonderful trips together, and so on. Unfortunately, no one is perfect, and it's unlikely that any relationship will be without problems and conflicts. Avoid complaining instead of dreaming. Don't comment on how your second spouse is not as affectionate as you had hoped; don't make remarks about how you don't have that much sex any more or how you never go anywhere. The motto of the second marriage should be the motto of the British Secret Service: Never complain; never explain.

Accept That Dreams Don't Come True

The likelihood of your dream coming true is not great. If you feel frustrated, change the dream. Perhaps you were marrying someone whom you thought would be very affectionate. You were mistaken. Dream about how your spouse is a wonderful cook instead. You thought you would spend all this time together. Dream about how wonderful it is to be married to someone that is so driven that work never stops. Try to match your dream to what is possible and real.

Avoid Entering the Second Marriage with a Plan for Divorce

If you enter the second marriage with a plan about how you are not going to lose anything in the second divorce, you are setting yourself up for a self-fulfilling prophecy, and there may actually be a second divorce. Try to preserve your innocence and assume that the second marriage will last forever.

If You Want a Prenuptial Agreement, Include a Gift

Sometimes a situation can be so complicated in terms of children from previous marriages and other commitments that a prenuptial agreement is necessary. You must understand that the point of making most prenuptial agreements is to ensure that your spouse will not gain any material wealth from the marriage. This is not a good start. So, if you must make the agreement, include a gift. As part of the prenuptial agreement, give a significant gift to your spouse, so he or she doesn't feel rejected or in some way disinherited before the marriage even starts.

Choose Carefully and Avoid Trying to Change Your Spouse

Beware of two issues. First, you are the same person you were with your first spouse, so your second spouse, living with you, will tend to become more and more similar to your first spouse. Second, the tendency in the second marriage is to grab the role that your spouse had in the first marriage. If this happens, your second spouse will develop all the bad qualities that you had in your first marriage. Choose carefully so you don't end up married for the second time to the same person or someone who is exactly like yourself. Otherwise, you'll once again find yourself trying to change your spouse, which takes too much time and energy and is ultimately futile.

Negotiate Fairly

Make a common pot and decide jointly who is going to put how much into this pot. Whether you decide on a fixed amount or a percentage, make sure that the decision takes into account each spouse's personal situation with regard to work, family obligations and children from previous marriages.

Everyone hopes to have a wonderful first and second marriage. If your marriage suffers from any of the problems described at the beginning of this chapter, the steps proposed at the end may help. If you are about to enter a second marriage, the steps will be useful in having a fresh start.

In this chapter, we have looked at some of the specific problems of second marriages. We'll now go on to see how money also has secret meanings in a variety of family situations: in wealth and poverty. In the next chapter, we will address some of the issues related to deprivation in the family.

Chapter Seven

When Parents Are Impoverished

Family members typically behave in covert ways under the stress of poverty. When a parent loses a job and the family becomes impoverished, everyone suffers in various ways. The worst pain may not be just the deprivation that is the natural consequence of impoverishment but the possibility that parents will often take out their frustrations on the children and become abusive. Yet even abuse may not be as painful to some children as watching their parents suffer and not being able to help.

In times of need, everyone in the family must help. Such a strong belief that it's wrong for children to take care of their parents prevails in the United States, however, that there are few ways in which children can actually help. Even when they do help, we often prefer to deny that they are taking care of us, and we do not offer appreciation. The problem is how to recognize when our children are helping us and show appreciation for their help.

Taking Care of Parents

The parents of Jennifer, a sixteen-year-old, came to see me because they said she was out of control. She went out too much, they didn't like her friends, she didn't help with the chores, and she didn't help the mother, who was chronically ill with multiple sclerosis.

Jennifer was the adoptive daughter of the mother and her first husband, who had been divorced. Her adoptive father had died recently, and the mother had remarried. The stepfather had been out of work for one year, and the family was in serious financial trouble. The mother came to see me alone at first and mentioned that the family was staying afloat thanks to the social security check that was coming to Jennifer because of her father's death.

At first, Jennifer refused to come to see me. Jennifer held three jobs, went to school, and didn't have time for therapy. When she finally came, I met with her alone. She was a Madonna look-alike, posturing as a defiant, rebellious adolescent.

Trying to show that I was willing to hear her point of view, I asked, "I was wondering if there are some things in your family that you are concerned about, that you would like to change?"

"If you want my family to come in, I will bring in my family. If you want the people out in the waiting room, then you can let them in," Jennifer answered haughtily.

"What do you mean?" I asked.

"They're not my family," she answered condescendingly.

"Who is your family?" I asked.

"My friends," she answered, savoring the word.

I thought that it was typically adolescent to feel so strongly about her friends, but her rejection of her family seemed too extreme.

She spoke angrily but tearfully, and slowly, I pieced together that she worked all these jobs because the family had no money. She paid all her expenses from the money that she herself made.

"Do you get any allowance from your parents, Jennifer?" I asked.

"They don't have any money," she answered, impatient with me for asking the obvious.

"So you work . . . ," I started to ask.

"That's . . . why . . . I . . . have . . . three . . . jobs," Jennifer interrupted indignantly, "because . . . they . . . don't . . . have . . . any . . . money," she continued. "To keep myself alive, to keep myself together, to feed myself, that is what I need to do."

Jennifer thought of herself as an orphan, alone in the world, no one to care for her, when in fact, she not only had parents, but she was supporting them.

Talking About Money

I brought the parents into the room. The mother, small and frail, had a look of vague, helpless incompetence. The father, rough and angry, appeared to be bigger than he actually was. I said, "I would like to resolve some issues regarding money or at least talk about them."

The stepfather snapped, "What are you talking about?"

"I know money is very limited," I said. "Also, I know that Jennifer doesn't have any regular allowance. I know that she's working a great deal, which is very commendable. She's very responsible. I would like to see whether we could find some way to get Jennifer some regular allowance money that is not dependent on her holding three jobs while she's going to school."

I was talking about an allowance for Jennifer when what I really wanted to talk about was how the parents were using her social security check. The subject of this check, however, was delicate, because the mother had told me about it when the stepfather was not present. I was afraid that if I revealed the source of my information, the stepfather would be angry at the mother for telling me.

The stepfather turned to Jennifer, "Do you want to tell her what you get an allowance for doing?"

"The dishes and the kitchen floor," answered Jennifer.

"Want to tell her how many times you've done it?" asked the stepfather.

"You want to talk about how many times I've been home to do it?" asked Jennifer.

"No," said the stepfather, "how many times you've done it."

"I don't stay there," said Jennifer. "I don't eat there; I don't do anything there. So I'm never around to do any chores. Not to mention that Mom told me you can't afford to pay me any allowance for doing chores anyway."

"So why give an allowance to somebody who's not there?" The stepfather was addressing me, but then he turned to Jennifer. "So tell me if I'm not right. You're not there, you don't contribute, so why should you do any chores?"

I answered the stepfather. "I think it's really important at this time to try to establish some fair distribution of resources in the family and to find out where the resources are going now.

We need to see if there is any way that we can make things fairer."

The mother said, "Fairness doesn't come into it right now."

"I hear that too," I said, and then asked the parents to confirm that they were keeping the money that came to Jennifer from social security.

The stepfather said, "If right now we gave Jennifer the money she's getting from social security, I'd be declaring bankruptcy the minute I walked out of here."

"I hear that," I said.

"That's no joke," continued the stepfather.

"I know that," said Jennifer, obviously upset at the subject of conversation.

The stepfather raised his voice, turning to Jennifer. "I don't know who the hell brought this up in the first place!" He was angry and threatening to the girl for having revealed the situation to me. "You bring this up?" he added.

"I told her we don't have any money," answered Jennifer.

"I brought it up," I said, "because this social security check comes to Jennifer because her father died. It's really hers."

"Mm-hmm," said the stepfather.

"And perhaps she should be getting the whole check and maybe paying you rent or paying you something for her expenses," I added.

"Why do you raise this issue?" asked the stepfather.

"With your permission I'm going to be very frank," I said. "You told me that if her check didn't go to you, you would have to declare bankruptcy."

"That's a fact," said the stepfather.

"I'm worried . . . ," I started to say, but the stepfather interrupted me.

"I'm considering bankruptcy right now," he said, turning angrily once more toward Jennifer. "Is that what you want?"

"No, I don't want anything to do with it," said Jennifer.

I waved my hand in front of the stepfather to get his attention, and, pointing with both hands to my own chest, I said, "It's me. This is my concern. She needs to stay out of it. It's my concern."

Supporting the Family

Money—who gives it to whom, who uses it to protect whom, and who doesn't want to talk about it—is difficult to understand if the family doesn't cooperate. At this point, I had realized that Jennifer's undone chores were not the issue. The issue was that the parents were pretending that Jennifer was a typical rebellious adolescent daughter when, in fact, she was supporting the family as if she were an adult. There were three pretenders in the family.

Pretender 1 was the mother, weak and sick, who wanted to be protected by both her husband and Jennifer. She collaborated with the stepfather in keeping Jennifer's money while pretending that this wasn't happening or that, if it was happening, it was a normal thing to do.

The stepfather was Pretender 2. He pretended to be interested in disciplining Jennifer in order to cover up for the fact that he was keeping her money, while silencing everyone with threats of bankruptcy. Also, the threat that he might abandon the mother was tacitly present in every interaction. Looking at them, I could see that he was strong and still young, while she was prematurely aging and quite ill. The stepfather also pretended that the recession had hit him so hard it was impossible for him to get any kind of job, when in fact this was not true.

Finally, Pretender 3: Jennifer loved her mother and wanted to protect her, so she had to live with her. In order to live with her, she had to pretend that she was childish and in need of protection, so she discussed chores and allowances, which was quite absurd given the fact that she was the only one who worked and brought money home. She also had to pretend to ignore that her mother and stepfather were spending the money from her inheritance. In order to keep the rule, imposed by the stepfather, that money should not be talked about, she had to keep silent and withdraw from the parents. Pretending to be rebellious, she could avoid conversation of all sorts and thus ensure that issues about money would not come out.

An outsider can be totally deceived by the way a family presents itself. Looking at this family superficially, the father seemed strong and competent; the mother, though sickly, was loving; and Jennifer was an obnoxious, rebellious, adolescent girl, who overdid the part by looking so much like Madonna.

Money and Hierarchy

When presented with the problem of a rebellious adolescent, my goal as a therapist is usually to restore the parents' authority over the young person. Parents are supposed to protect and guide their children until they become adults, and they need to have the authority to be able to do so. In fact, since society holds parents responsible for their adolescent children, there is an implicit hierarchy in every family in which parents have more power than their children.

Sometimes, however, an adolescent can rebel and frighten the parents so that a dual hierarchy is defined in the family. On the one hand, the parents are in a superior position because they have legal power and are responsible for the adolescent; on the other hand, the youth dominates the parents by frightening them with threats or with extreme behaviors. The job of the therapist is to empower the parents to be in charge once again of the young person. This task is done by helping the parents set rules for the young person and consequences if the rules are disobeyed, and by helping them stick to these rules and consequences in spite of the youth's efforts to break them.

In Jennifer's case, I could not arrange for a traditional hierarchy in which the parents would be in charge of their daughter in typical ways, making her do chores, paying her an allowance, and expecting her to be grateful that she had parents who could take care of her. The reality was that Jennifer worked hard and sup-ported the family, while the parents didn't work and bring in any money. To pretend that the parents could be in charge would have been to collude with their deception and their refusal to face the truth about where the money was coming from. Lies and deception are never conducive to a positive family life.

What I could do was to encourage the family to put all the cards on the table and speak openly about how Jennifer's money was used and how hard she worked. They had to face the fact that it was absurd to expect her to do chores when she had three jobs and they didn't work, just as it was absurd to think that the allowance was coming from anywhere else than from the money she herself brought into the family.

I couldn't change the fact that Jennifer's father had died, that she had an inheritance that her parents had used, and that she needed to work. What I could do was to get the parents to acknowledge openly that this was the case and show appreciation to Jennifer for what she was doing. If Jennifer received this appre-ciation, she could drop the deception and with it her rebellious pos-ture, which was totally out of character for a young girl who was so generous and self-sacrificing.

I also realized that Jennifer was very fearful that the stepfather might abandon her mother. She cared so much for her mother that she was willing to support the family to make sure that the stepfa-ther stayed. I had to be very careful not to do anything that would threaten the stability of the parents' marriage. For this reason, I had to let Jennifer continue to refuse to talk about money. I had to take it upon myself that I was curious about this topic, not Jennifer. I had to make sure that the parents would not quarrel with each other, and I had to help them save face.

In this scenario I was the fourth pretender. The parents had consulted me to solve the problem of Jennifer's rebellion. They hadn't asked me to discuss their financial situation. I had to pretend that I was helping them understand and control their daughter, while in fact I was negotiating for Jennifer to get some appreciation and have a better situation at home. The father's rule of silence didn't apply to me, so I could pretend to be curious about money issues. I could pretend to expect that they would talk to a therapist about everything, including money. So one by one I started to remove the strings attached to money issues.

The Dollar Figure

I waved my hand in front of the stepfather as I said, "This is my concern."

"So," said the stepfather, "where the hell is this going, anyhow? You think I should just give her her social security check and say, 'You owe me $800 a month to live here'?"

This was the first time that a dollar amount had been mentioned. I suspected that this was the amount of Jennifer's social security check.

"I think we need to talk about it," I said. "That's all I'm saying. I need to find out where the money is coming from and where it's going and what might be a better way to restructure things."

Jennifer interrupted, "They have to pay bills to stay in the house. That's why they get it. That's why I work," she said emphatically.

"She's giving what is her father's inheritance," I continued, "to help the family. She's been doing that, and also she's working, providing for her own needs. She is an incredibly generous person."

"Jenny," said the mother tenderly, as she took Jennifer's hand warmly.

"I think she's really concerned," I said. "She didn't tell me this, but I think she's really concerned that the family doesn't have adequate resources at this time. She's really worried about it, and she's being extremely generous. It's not the time, at the moment, to be all that critical of her because she's showing a whole lot of gen-erosity to the family. That's the way I see it."

"OK," said the stepfather, "so because she's putting in money to keep us all afloat, we should overlook a lot of things." His tone was ironic.

"No," I said, "that's not what I'm saying. What I'm saying is that it's maybe not the time to be demanding a whole lot of her, for example, to make her do chores in exchange for an allowance. It's not as if you can say, 'Jennifer, you're not giving me anything so I won't give you anything.' She's already giving you a lot."

"What are you asking us to do?" said the stepfather indignantly. "What do you want me to do? It's her money. Do you want me to give it to her? What do you want? What do you think I should do with it, give it to her?"

"What do you think you should do with it?" I asked. "And how much is it? This is a matter that we need to discuss together."

"It's $321.05," said the stepfather. He was not mentioning two facts, which I knew from Jennifer's mother. First, there was a lump sum of Jennifer's inheritance that the parents had taken. Second, the Social Security Administration had made a mistake and over-paid for many months; now it was compensating by sending a much smaller check for a while.

Acknowledging a Loan

My next step was to find out on what conditions the mother and stepfather had taken Jennifer's money. Was it a loan? Was it a gift? Was it an obligation? Did they think the money was rightfully theirs? I was certain that the money was truly Jennifer's, and I decided to work toward an agreement that it was a loan that Jennifer was making to her parents.

"I wonder how much of the money goes to pay for Jennifer's own living expenses," I said, "and how much it is money that could be considered borrowed from her."

"What do you mean?" asked the father.

"I mean that some of that money might be thought of as being borrowed from Jennifer, and some of it is obviously her expenses," I said.

"If it's borrowed money," said the father, "then I ought to pay her interest on it, fairly."

"Right," I said, pleasantly surprised. "That's something that we could discuss."

"That's the money that they need to pay things," said Jennifer anxiously. "I don't want it."

I decided to show some empathy for the stepfather. "In times when you're making good money," I said, "and when the economy is good, parents support children. When times get really tough, some of that breaks down. In this case, you've been lucky because Jennifer has been able to contribute in this way. I think there needs to be a certain expression of gratitude for that." I knew that it would be difficult for the stepfather to express gratitude, so I had softened my request with some expression of sympathy for his plight.

"I agree," said the stepfather, "but to participate in a family is not just monetary value. There were times before when I got laid off the job and I never touched her money. It was there."

I wondered what he meant by monetary value and what money was there to take in the past, but I decided to restrain my curiosity and stay focused on what I wanted the stepfather to do. I said, "Sure, I understand."

"If I hadn't been laid off and I was making money," said the stepfather, "I would still probably be here. The money has very damned little to do with it."

I understood that what the stepfather was trying to do was convince me that he did not stay with Jennifer's mother for the money. He was responding to an accusation that I had not made.

"I hear you saying that you have been a good supporter of the family for a long time," I said, "and you're going through a really difficult period. It's a period where all of a sudden things get turned around. All of a sudden, Jennifer's out making her own money and you're borrowing some of hers. And that's OK, but there has to be some acknowledgment of what that situation is, some sense of, 'My goodness! We're lucky to have this!'"

"OK," said the stepfather.

"And I believe that the money owed Jennifer is considerably more than what the figure you gave me would reflect," I said.

"Probably," said the stepfather, "yeah."

"And it's money that could have been saved for a college education," I said, "or to make a down payment on a house, or for whatever she might need it in the future."

The stepfather asked, "What you're saying is that she feels unappreciated for what she's doing?"

Jennifer said, "I have nothing to do with this."

"That is my interpretation," I said, "not hers."

"It has absolutely nothing to do with me," said Jennifer.

"And I think," I continued, "it would be helpful if you thanked her."

Giving Thanks

"I don't care," said Jennifer.

"In spite of the fact of what she's saying," I continued, "that she doesn't care, I think it's important."

The mother spoke, "It never occurred to me to say thank you, to tell you the truth, but we do as much as we can for Jennifer."

"I understand that," I said. "But maybe she deserves a thank you."

"Thank you," whispered the mother to Jennifer.

"Money buys anything, right?" said the stepfather to Jennifer, who giggled half-tearfully.

"It doesn't matter to me," said Jennifer emphatically. She had been repeating that money was unimportant and not a worthy subject of conversation for the whole hour.

"Can you say thank you?" I asked the stepfather.

Jennifer said, "He just did in his own little way. It doesn't matter to me."

I marveled at how family members understand each other, even when messages are quite incomprehensible for an outsider. When the stepfather had said, 'Money buys everything,' the girl had understood his statement to mean that he was thanking her. It was possible to consider the message a tongue-in-cheek way of saying that he appreciated her not just for the money, but this was an interpretation that would not have occurred to me. In any case, indirect expressions of appreciation were not good enough. The stepfather had to thank Jennifer explicitly.

"It hasn't been quite good enough for me," I said.

"Well, I'm sorry," said Jennifer, "'cause I know my stepfather, OK? It doesn't matter to me one way or another. When I tell you something doesn't matter, it's plain and simple—it doesn't matter. You should drop it."

I said, "Would you say thank you to her?"

Jennifer said loudly, "Would you please stop?"

The stepfather spoke over her, looking at me threateningly, "Don't push me now. Don't push."

"I am pushing," I said. "I think it's very important."

Again, the mother said softly, "Thank you, Jennifer."

The stepfather said, "Jennifer, I thank you." He had tears in his eyes.

"Thank you," said Jennifer to her stepfather, "but see . . ."

I interrupted, "That sounded very sincere."

Jennifer continued addressing me. "See, there's something that I need to inform you. You're not listening!"

"I'm talking to your father right now," I said. "I think it's very hard to raise children in difficult economic times. I think it's very, very difficult. I think you guys have been doing a really good job." Now that the stepfather had finally thanked Jennifer, I wanted to praise him and help him save face, after what for him must have been an ordeal of humiliation.

The stepfather said, "I think it's a lousy job, if you want my opinion of it. It's nowhere near where I think it should be, and I'm not happy with it. Actually, I'm a very unfriendly person when you start talking finances. The financial situation is a problem that I would prefer not to . . . I'm going to handle it. I would prefer that Jennifer take care of her school work and get her life on line."

I said, "What I hear you saying is that you're going to handle the finances. That's your job, and I commend you for that. It's really important. I think you guys have done a very commendable job getting through this difficult situation."

Finding a Job

A week later the stepfather had found a job and was working. He had realized that in difficult economic times one sometimes needs to come down one level in order to find work. He had given up trying to find a job as a manager and had accepted a regular job instead. Remarkably, all three were getting along, the parents were very interested and encouraging of the girl's activities, and the girl behaved as if they had always been a close, loving family.

Perhaps the stepfather had suddenly been able to find a job because in having to thank Jennifer, he felt that he was losing his superior position in the family hierarchy. He may have decided to choose a lower-level job and lose some of his position in the work hierarchy, in order to regain his standing with the family.

Being a Child Again

Jennifer could now think of her parents once more as her family, because she had regained her position in the family hierarchy as a daughter instead of living in the confusing situation in which she was supposed to be a child but was supporting the family. Jennifer had abruptly changed from being on the receiving end as a child, while her father was alive, to being on the giving end, supporting the family. This abrupt change was unfavorable to her. Removing the confusion about whether the money was a gift or a loan and talking explicitly about money issues and gratefulness made it possible for Jennifer to recover her position as a child.

Generosity

Jennifer's parents had responded to her generosity with resentment. When they consulted me, they were full of complaints about their daughter and seemed to have little, if any, appreciation of her. I was able to convince them of Jennifer's generosity and the need to respond with appreciation and gratitude.

Generosity often breeds resentment. The logical response to generosity would seem to be gratitude, yet this rarely happens. The generous often are envied and resented. This response happens for several reasons. First, we all admire those who can be generous. For many of us, it's very difficult to admire other people, because we dislike to acknowledge the superiority of others. While it's very difficult to feel admiration, it's easier to feel envy. So we often resent those whom we truly admire. We resent the very generosity that makes them superior.

Second, the person who receives a generous offering may respond with feelings of humiliation, thinking that the gift implies that one has less, that the other has more. This situation is the breeding ground for resentment.

For these reasons, those who are focused on giving rather than receiving often feel unloved. No matter how much they give, perhaps precisely because they give, they are resented. Many problems in families can be solved when people recognize that they have no reason for resentment and can transform their resentment into gratefulness.

The Emotional Economy of Impoverishment

There are two kinds of economy relating to money: one is financial; the other is emotional. The emotional economy of impoverishment is quite different from that of wealth. Frustration, sadness, hostility, and resentment are the characteristic emotions in impoverished families. Often these emotions are misdirected. When a father loses his job, his hostility and resentment may be directed toward a child instead of his employer, as was the case of Jennifer's stepfather.

In poverty, emotions are misdirected because family relations are altered. Parents are supposed to provide for their children. When they are not able to do so, their position in the family and society is undermined.

Children naturally want to help their parents, but they are faced with the problem that if they do so, they are undermining the parents even more because they are taking care of them instead of the normal way around. This was Jennifer's problem, so she was taking care of the parents while pretending that she was not and while insisting that she didn't even like them—"They are not my family." The parents collaborated in this pretense, and the pretense itself contributed to the father's inability to find a new job.

When Jennifer's help was recognized and appreciated, the emotional economy of the family was corrected, and the father was able to find a job and provide once more for the family.

Just as there are secret meanings and covert behavior regarding money in families with poverty, so there are covert and hidden ways people use money in families with wealth, which is the subject of the next chapter.

Chapter Eight

Problems of a Wealthy Family

The passing of money from one generation to the next is a problem for many families, especially in a society in which it's relatively easy to go up or down in social class. Sometimes a person will rise from poverty and become wealthy, but the wealth will last only one generation. The children will not obtain the necessary education, they will not be able to preserve the wealth, and they will come down to the social class and poverty from which the parent started.

Most parents want their children to do at least as well as themselves and even to surpass their accomplishments. But some parents use money in covert ways to undermine their children. They seem to secretly arrange for their children to fail financially. This is a sort of antithesis of the American dream in which the next generation is always better off than the previous one.

How Not to Give

Some of the ways in which parents give to their children encourage them to grow and enhance their self-esteem. Other ways of giving discourage the children, stunt their growth, and misdirect them. The more wealthy the family, the easier it is to give in the wrong way.

"I've been an asshole to my wife again," said Bruce matter-of-factly as he entered the therapy room. He looked filthy in his tattered blue jeans and old T-shirt, long hair; he was unshaven, indifferent.

Bruce had been court ordered to therapy for various offenses, including marital violence, multiple counts of driving under the influence, possession of narcotics with intent to distribute, evading child support, and attempted murder. He was an expert motorcycle racer, with several national awards.

"A Hemingway character!" I thought to myself. My work as a therapist has hardened me to most of life's problems. This afternoon had been the usual succession of unhappy couples and rebellious adolescents with desperate parents. I was bored, but suddenly I became alert. Bruce was out of the ordinary.

"I'm twenty-nine years old," said Bruce.

He appeared to be over forty. I realized this would be a particularly difficult case. "What losses, other than motorcycle races, had Bruce suffered that were reflected in his prematurely aging face?" was the first question I began to formulate in my mind.

Losses

To understand someone's losses, we first need to inquire about the person's accomplishments. Losses are only losses in relation to what could have been gained. I realized I had to address Bruce's accomplishments before I could talk about his losses. I thought that I could put his accomplishments in terms of courage. He was a risk taker who reminded me of Hemingway's story "The Killers." I had known some boxers and automobile racers who were similar to him. What I didn't know then was that in Bruce was that mixture of Hemingway's ambivalence about the wealthy together with his fascination with risk takers.

As I thought about this, I felt a rush of adrenaline. I was excited about Bruce. Even though he seemed nothing more than a skid row bum, I told him he looked like a brave person, someone who had done some pretty heroic things.

"I've done a few brave things," agreed Bruce, pleased at the compliment, "but I've always had trouble with women. Once I beat this guy up and took his bitch with me," he said proudly. "She left me three or four times. I paid for her plane every time she wanted to go, then she would come back. Finally one day she took all my money and left for good. Months later she came back crying that she was pregnant, and I got back with her."

"A complicated way of being kind," I thought. I could picture Bruce paying for the plane tickets in order to be abandoned, paying for another ticket when the woman changed her mind, and finally taking her back when she was pregnant by another man. What was this guy doing to himself?

"How long have you been racing bikes?" I asked.

"Always," said Bruce. "My dad used to race cars. I had to go to the track with him. I had a dirt bike." He looked younger as he talked about his childhood. "I grew up riding dirt bikes and motorcycles. My dad wanted me to learn to race cars one day, ever since I was a baby." Bruce's tone became nostalgic as he continued sadly. "He raced cars until I was sixteen, then I ran way from home. When I came back one month later, he had sold the race car and everything." He paused before continuing. "My whole life was getting yelled at and knocked around and screamed at in front of people at the racetrack, in front of his buddies. I'd get the wrong wrench and he'd scream and cuss at me."

There was no anger in Bruce, only sadness. "And then he sells the car so I could never be a car racer. That's a rift I have with my dad. I want to smack him in the head or something. I was the only one that wanted to be a car racer like him. My oldest brother went into the military; my other brother was a biker drug addict. He didn't want no part in it, so it came down to me. And I enjoyed it."

As Bruce related the story of his racing, he was defining his father's personality. "Another asshole?" I thought. "What kind of father pushes his son into a career as a car racer, only to sell the car and frustrate the desire that he himself had created?" At this point I took for granted that the father was a worse bum than Bruce.

Family Ties

"Do you keep in touch with your brothers and sisters?" I asked.

"No, not really. We're all fucked up, every one of us, except my oldest brother, and I don't see him any more."

Apparently Bruce's delinquency was a common trait in his family, where the chief example of being an ass seemed to be the father. In most families, one child performs the function of the problem kid while the others are free to be successful. In this case, it seemed that most of the children were problems, the exception being the oldest, who left for the army at sixteen.

Bruce continued to relate how alcoholism, drug abuse, and physical abuse figured into the life of each sibling. As I listened to Bruce's story, I took for granted that the next thing I would hear would be how the father was destitute or seriously ill. Many years of experience have taught me that the antisocial behaviors that Bruce described in himself and his siblings often stem from the despair of not being able to help a parent who is impoverished or dying.

"How has your father been doing?" I asked.

To my surprise, Bruce answered, "He's done really well. He makes something like three hundred thousand a year."

"From what?" I asked, surprised.

"From his job. He's the marketing director of [a Fortune 500 corporation]."

"I'm surprised. Do you stand to inherit a lot of money?" I was trying to figure out the implications of this new information.

"I don't think so. I'd just as soon write him a letter and tell him to forget I'm his son."

"You would?" I was surprised again as Bruce expressed his willingness to disinherit himself.

"Yeah," replied Bruce. "And, by the way, he's paying for this therapy."

Using Money to Teach Lessons

I scratched my head. Why didn't Bruce want his father's money? One could possibly expect such refusal from a successful young man who wants to make the point that he can make it on his own.

But from a failed delinquent drug dealer? Why wouldn't he take his father's money? I remembered how Bruce had said that his siblings were also failures, and I thought, "This can't be the work of only one generation. It takes more than one generation to produce this kind of failure." Bruce represented the existential dilemma better than any of the Hemingway characters. Could I find him in Sartre's books?

I woke up from my reverie when I heard Bruce say, "My wife thinks I'm gonna get a lot of money because my uncle has a lot of money, and my grandmother has quite a bit too. She's given me a lot of money through the years. And my dad's helped me out in predicaments. He bought me a house, and I was supposed to pay him rent, which I really didn't because I was doing drugs and drinking. My dad is just sick of everybody. I used to call him up whenever I got in trouble and needed money. The others did the same."

"The fact that this motorcycle-racing tough-guy felon is the son of a successful man explains a lot about Bruce," I thought as he went on to complain about how much his father always talked about having two or three jobs and working his way through school. The father had lived the American dream, having worked his way from poverty into wealth. He was also generous and had given a considerable amount of money to his mother. A common dilemma for this type of person is that in order to feel understood by their children, they want to teach them the meaning of poverty, and by extension, money and struggle. This wish leads to a preoccupation with not spoiling or pampering their children and a habit of constantly testing or challenging them in order to foster an independent spirit. The danger is that the child often perceives this idea of education as hostile and demeaning, violating the parent-child contract that parents should protect and help their children since the world will provide obstacles enough.

This type of conflict usually comes to a head during adolescence, when hostilities and rebellion become overt. In Bruce's case, his father brought him up to be a racer, which is abnormal in that most parents want their children to attain or surpass the socioeconomic level of their upbringing and usually don't encourage children into life-threatening careers. Second, the father's violence turned his wishes for Bruce into a point of contention between them. However, by punishing an adolescent in such a severe and irreparable form as to sell all the racing equipment, he made permanent the rebellion and hostility of adolescence, since Bruce was then equally unable to race or enter business.

When there is such resentment, it's common to develop a symptom rather than split with a parent. Thus, when his father gave him a house, with the condition of paying rent—which prevented it from serving as a full-fledged reparation—Bruce failed the conditions. Since the father didn't manage to give help directly and since the son didn't know how to ask, the son had cost the father more than the price of a college education in bail, legal expenses, hospital bills, overdue rent and mortgage payments, and various other emergencies.

The Power of Impoverishment

It's easy to see how money is power. Those who have money have power over those who don't. Money makes it possible to help others and also to corrupt with bribes, create dependency, and buy love and respect. We all start life as children when we don't have anything and our parents have everything. We are totally dependent on our parents. Some parents encourage this dependence, feeling that the only way they can keep their children's love and respect is through money. Yet most of us are able to establish our own sources of income and love our parents irrespective of the material things they can give us.

Sometimes a child so resents a parent that the natural process of separation becomes secondary to another main goal. The child wants revenge. To hurt the parent becomes more important than anything else in life. The parent has to pay. But the child also loves the parent.

Caught in this ambivalence, the adolescent or young adult thinks that the best way to hurt the parent is by hurting him- or herself. If the young person fails in life, cannot even make a living, is always impoverished no matter how much money is received from the family, surely that will make the parent suffer. Also, impoverishment will ensure an enduring relationship with the parent who will continue to have everything while the child has nothing. Impoverishment gives power in that it condemns the parent to always give. Going down in social class means always staying on the receiving end.

Everybody Has Something to Give

The usual way in which children grow up and separate from the family is with the encouragement of the parents, who gently push the children away from home. When this process is interrupted by conflicts and resentments and the young person stays in a dependent relationship longer than normal, the parent can start again and do all that could have been done in the past to help and encourage the young person. However, when the young person has been stuck for many years in a situation of failure, it's best for the youth to have the experience of giving before getting out of the receiving end.

Up to now, Bruce had experienced giving by caring for the women in his life. The circuit of money was from the father to Bruce to Bruce's women. Bruce could give only to those he felt were beneath him. Now, however, he had to experience giving to those he felt were above him. If he could do that, feeling at the same level as his father, he would be able to separate from him.

The major focus of Bruce's life had been to obtain help and money from his family. Now he needed to experience the act of giving, but before doing anything in this regard I needed to know more about the family.

"Who is someone in your life that was really there for you, through thick and thin, somebody who you really admired?" I asked.

"That I could call for help, someone to talk to?" Bruce answered his own question in the way I expected: "Well, my dad."

I was sure there had to be others. "Your dad has been there through thick and thin?" I asked.

"Yeah, he gets frustrated with me because I keep doing dumb shit. My aunt's been there, my sister's been there, my mother . . ."

I hadn't expected so many helpers.

"Was she the real mother of mothers?" I continued to ask. "Was she the one who was always there for you?"

"My grandmother . . . she was as much a mother to me as my mom." Bingo! I thought that Bruce had now identified the central person.

"My dad's mom," he continued. "Like when I got hurt and was in the hospital for surgery, it was pretty bad, and my grandmother was there. My dad, he didn't really want to go. He was more disgusted with me than anything. I've always had my grandmother, though."

"She was there for you," I said, "someone who took care of you throughout your life."

"She still tries to." Bruce's expression and tone of voice had softened in talking about his grandmother.

Giving Instead of Receiving

I thought, "The old lady must love to have the love of her grandson, even though he is always taking from her." I wondered whether I could get Bruce to give something to his grandmother and by doing so begin to change his relationship with the whole family.

But what to give an old lady? Often the elderly are involved in charities and volunteer work. If Bruce helped the grandmother by giving to those she cared for, he would also be giving to her and I would accomplish my purpose. Maybe I could develop a bond between the two based on generosity.

What would take me by surprise was to discover that that bond already existed.

"Does your grandmother donate time or money to certain causes, such as hungry children or . . . ?"

Before I could finish my question, Bruce interrupted, "She used to care for the elderly. I used to go up there all the time when I was little."

"You did?" I asked with surprise. "When was the last time you were up there?"

"I believe before I was a teenager, eleven or twelve."

"I think that you have some of your grandmother's compassion," I said. "She devoted a portion of her life to helping the elderly."

"I used to work with the mentally handicapped," said Bruce.

"You did? That's terrific!"

"The court sentenced me to community service, and I was going to do just something dumb, and then my lawyer told me about this."

"Did you enjoy it?" I asked.

"Yeah," said Bruce with nostalgia. "I kind of wish I could go back to see them people and do it some more."

"That's exactly what I had in mind," I said.

For a brief moment Bruce had revealed a suppressed aspect of his personality, the Bruce that wanted to help others. But this was a fleeting moment. He didn't want to be in the position of being a generous person who gives, for fear of losing his position with his own family as the one who always is on the receiving end. So, with his next statement, he went back to his old self.

"I don't have time, and I can't get around," he said. (His driver's license had been revoked.) "It was neat, though," he continued. "I liked it. They were like my age, but mentally they weren't. Physically I could kind of relate to them, but it was funny."

"If I were to ask you two things that you enjoyed most about that time, what would they be?" I asked.

"Just spending time with them people, teaching them. They're neat people." There was tenderness in Bruce's voice. "I got a soft heart in a way, though most people wouldn't know it. Like Debbie knows, and my ex-wife knows, because they've seen me break down and cry; they've seen me get upset. You know, I've attempted suicide. I've done some weird shit, and these people are aware of the things I've done in my life. There's a couple other close friends, but most people wouldn't think I'm that type of guy. They think I'm an asshole."

"Well, there's that key word again," I said, remembering how Bruce had started the session.

Countering Self-Deprecation

I thought about how this type of self-deprecating remark is a way of shunning any responsibility. If Bruce were an asshole, then nothing could be expected of him. In order to become a responsible adult, Bruce had to think of himself as such, not as an asshole.

Bruce continued. "I am an asshole, though! People tell me all the time, and I admit it—I agree. When people tell me I'm an asshole I say, 'So what?' Because I am."

I leaned forward in my chair. "I put it to you that not many assholes could sit here and talk to me with such tenderness about these people that you worked with."

"Yeah," conceded Bruce, "but that's just a separate part of me, though."

"That's the part of you that I'm talking to," I said.

I sighed with relief; now I was talking to a Bruce who was kind, compassionate, and intelligent.

Back to the Great Dilemma

In Chapter Two, I described how one of the greatest dilemmas in our life is the transition from being cared for by our parents to taking care of our parents. In order to make this transition, the child needs to be able to help the parent. The parents who elicit the most serious pathology are those who don't allow the child to help them. Bruce had such a father.

In the beginning of the session, he had described how his father would insult him and reject him when he tried to help him at the racetrack. When someone cannot make the transition to adult life by helping a father, that person can do it by helping another older person in the family, in this case, the grandmother.

Anger

The despair of not being appreciated and not being able to help a parent typically leads to anger and violence. Bruce had been repeatedly violent toward others and himself. He desperately needed to control his anger.

"Bruce, you've talked about getting your anger under control," I said.

"It's always been a problem, even when I'm alone," answered Bruce.

"You've said that very clearly from the first time I met you," I said. "I want to talk about that right now."

Anger is a problem that has often been mishandled by therapists. A common belief in my line of work is that to express anger is somehow healthy. The idea is that one carries a certain amount of anger inside and to let it out is to get rid of it.

In fact, nothing could be further from the truth. The expression of anger only leads to more anger in oneself, and provokes anger and violence in others. An old Chinese proverb says, "When you kill in anger, dig two graves." I think that means that when we express anger, we always hurt ourselves as well as the other person and that no rightful or intelligent action can be carried out when experiencing anger. The only way to get rid of anger is by transforming it into a more positive emotion. But how to do this? One way is to change the object of the anger.

"Bruce, you are a sensitive person who understands human suffering and has gone through many difficulties," I said. "I suspect that one thing that is missing from your life is the possibility of doing something to correct some wrongdoing in the world, for example, helping the mentally retarded, who are so misunderstood. You found ways of communicating with them, and you worked with them long enough that you understand how there is another side to human beings, which is not necessarily the side we see first."

Bruce nodded in agreement.

"So I want to address that talent you have to reach another person's spirit. Instead of seeing yourself as always angry, as someone who can't feel for other people, as an asshole, I'd like you to do something different."

Bruce was interested in every word. He was wondering what I would suggest.

"Every time you start to feel like an asshole," I said, "is when you've done something wrong, like violence and drugs, or when you feel angry at yourself or at someone. There are going to be two things you will do when you begin to do something silly."

I had decided to use the word *silly* when referring to violence and substance abuse. It seemed a grandmotherly term, and I wanted to trigger Bruce's thoughts about his own grandmother. It would also take away any macho glamour associated with those behaviors.

"When you do something silly," I continued, "or when you begin to experience anger, I want you to call up one of the elderly agencies near you and see if there is anything you can do for them. Or you can call your grandmother and see what you can do for her. When you begin to feel anger about something stupid, like a quarrel with Debbie or what someone said, I want you to think about a good reason to be angry, like how badly the elderly or the mentally retarded are treated. Then you can be angry about something worthwhile and not about something silly."

Bruce listened attentively.

"Or you can do something nice for your grandmother," I added. "She is one of those elderly people that need attention. You can call her and say, 'I really miss you and would like to spend some time with you. How about I come by and we have a meal together or a cup of coffee?' You could go in a taxi, and she would be more than delighted to pay for the taxi, I'm sure."

"I could handle the taxi, probably. She wouldn't have to pay for it," said Bruce, apparently embarrassed by his situation.

Love

I had appealed to Bruce's sensitivity, and now he began to show his tenderness as he talked about his grandmother.

"She's paid enough," said Bruce. "She's given me thousands of dollars. If I call her up, she'll probably think I want money. It makes me feel bad. At Christmas time she called me up and said, 'I have some money for you.' I said, 'I don't want your money.' She said, 'Well, I'm going to give it to you anyway.' And I said, 'Well, I don't want it.' She said, 'I'll give it to you at your dad's house then.' And I said, 'Look, Nanny, I don't want your money!' She said, 'Don't you love me no more?' She thinks that just because I don't want her money I don't love her no more."

"Ah," I said, "she's a real grandmother, isn't she?"

"You know," said Bruce with regret, "I haven't been over there much lately, haven't talked to her much."

"See? So she'd like to see you," I said enthusiastically, "especially since you still call her 'Nanny.' You know, I suspect it was she who taught you how to have a heart."

"Yeah, she helped," said Bruce with emotion.

I sighed, relieved that I had found the tender heart behind the tough-guy facade.

Giving and Receiving

At this point, I began to discuss with Bruce the issue of giving and receiving money. Bruce was worried about the way he had approached his grandmother for money in the past and the possibility that she would undoubtedly suspect that he had come for more. The Christmas story he used as an example says something about the weight and power that money represented in this family, and about how Bruce's guilt feelings and anxiety about money worked to isolate him from them.

"If anybody found out how much money she's given me, I'd be killed, especially by my older brother. She's taken money out of other people's inheritances and given it to me. How do you think that makes me feel? And I would blow it and be calling her up begging for more."

"You're going to be calling her up for a different kind of help," I said. "You're going to say that you want to spend some time with her, which is a way of giving her back some of the things she's given you. Remember that every time you spend quality time with your grandmother, you are giving something back to her. How many years is she going to have to be able to have you come by and pay a friendly visit to her?"

"Not many," sighed Bruce.

"And if she wants to give you money," I continued, "you should take it. It will make her feel good, and it will make you feel better to accept a gift of love from your grandmother."

"I've blown it too many times!" Bruce shook his head.

"Well," I said, "it's a very special thing, a gift from a grandmother. Not everybody has such a generous grandma, and maybe you should show your appreciation by using her gift in the right way."

Giving in Order to Take

Some people give in order to be able to take back what they gave. This was the case of Bruce's father. He had encouraged Bruce in the career of racing only to take away the equipment. He had given Bruce the privilege of being his helper at the racetrack, only to yell and insult him in public. He had given him a house to live in but charged him rent. The result was that Bruce never knew whether he should be grateful or resentful.

In contrast, the grandmother did not expect anything in return from Bruce and gave to him without conditions about how Bruce should behave. The grandmother represented a consistent model of selfless giving. That is why Bruce would be able to give to his grandmother, without expecting anything in return.

"The gift of love that you get from your grandmother," I said, "is very special and should be treated differently. It's not the same as the money that you make from working."

"What do you mean?" asked Bruce.

"Well, maybe there should be some kind of ceremony when you get a gift of love, so that both you and she know that this isn't just ordinary money that she's given you. You know what I mean?"

"Yeah," said Bruce.

"So if she does give you money, put it in a safe place, and next week we can talk about an appropriate ceremony."

"OK."

"You should be happy about the goodness your grandmother puts out," I said. "Do you understand what I mean about your grandmother getting something in return just by your visit, even just by your phone call?"

"Do you think this is going to help my anger?" asked Bruce.

"Absolutely," I said. "You will transform the anger into a positive force. Not just by visiting your grandmother, but also because you are going to call that place you used to work for and ask them if you can drop in once in a while."

"They even sent me a shirt!" said Bruce with a certain pride.

"Oh, yeah? When?" I was happily surprised.

"A couple of months ago."

"That's incredible, Bruce," I said with admiration. "You left an impact. They didn't just scratch your name out of the Rolodex."

"Yeah, most people look at me and they want to," said Bruce, never missing an opportunity to put himself down.

Bruce started the next session by saying he had called not only his grandmother but also his father and two of his sisters during the last week. The conversations had been casual and friendly, with no mention or sign of past estrangement. He had argued once with his wife. When he called the center for the mentally impaired during off hours and failed to reach his grandmother, instead of raging, he took a walk to cool off. He had visited his grandmother, who gave him $200.

I proposed that the ceremony that I had mentioned should involve spending some of the money on a gift for his grandmother. After going over several possible presents, it was decided that half the money would buy her a lavish day at a beauty spa, including manicure, pedicure, facial, and massage. Bruce would put the other half in his bank account.

In later sessions, I discovered that Bruce's uncle, a wealthy man, had made Bruce a standing offer to give him $40,000 to start his own business. Bruce's father had responded competitively, also making an offer. He was probably reacting to the change in Bruce, who was now beginning to be proud of his interest in selfless giving. He was continuing to see his grandmother and was working part-time as a volunteer with the mentally impaired. In response to Bruce's generosity, the father was becoming more unconditionally giving.

Several sessions, including one with the father and uncle, were devoted to how ready Bruce was for such a big responsibility. After consulting with a financial adviser, Bruce decided to launch a business and created his own company with the help of his father and uncle.

In this chapter, we have looked at how parents can covertly use money to undermine their children. As we struggle to help our young adult children and to prevent them from failing financially, we are also aging. In the next chapter, we will look at the secret meaning and covert use of money by the older couple.

Chapter Nine

Money and the Older Couple

Most couples who have been together many years accumulate resentments that they play over and over in their minds like scenes from an old movie. These intrusive thoughts often appear against the person's will, blocking other thought processes. Obsessive resentments can force people to live in the past, interfering with the present and preventing couples from enjoying the good aspects of their relationship.

Resentments lead to estrangement and bad feeling, which in turn exacerbate whatever problems a couple might have. Old resentments often stem from the frustration of not having been loved and cherished as one would have wished. Although the past cannot be changed, our understanding of the meaning of the past can certainly be modified.

Extortion and the Threat of Divorce

Many couples stay together because a divorce would be too costly to one or both of them. Rather than suffer financial loss, they prefer to stay in a marriage that can only go from bad to worse if money is the reason for staying together. In marriage, the tie that binds must be love, not money.

With some couples, one spouse will habitually threaten divorce as a way of testing the commitment of the other spouse. The one that threatens divorce expects the other to offer reassurance and beg for love. To threaten divorce is a tactic similar to fishing for compliments. And like fishing for compliments, it can backfire.

For example, when a woman says, "I look awful today!" she probably expects her husband to reply with something like "You look very nice, dear." But sometimes a husband might say instead, "Yes, you really don't look well," which is very disconcerting to the woman expecting a compliment. It is the same with threats of divorce.

Some couples have a tacit agreement that the wife, for example, will threaten divorce and the husband will reassure her. The threat and the reassurance can be part of an interaction that repeats itself over many years, without any real possibility that the couple might actually separate. But life cannot always stay the same; change is inevitable. One day the husband might answer the threat by expressing that perhaps a separation would be better, and then the couple is in crisis.

It was a crisis of this kind that brought Margaret and Carl to a therapist. They had been married for thirty years and were in such disagreement about money that they were about to get a divorce.

As Margaret put it, "We have a terminal relationship. I think the only thing that keeps the marriage together is money. There is no love. We should either divorce and get out of this stress, or we should go on to these golden years and be happier." This seemed reasonable enough. She added, "My husband says he's not unhappy. But I'm certainly not happy myself."

"That's not what I said," interjected Carl.

"What did you say?" asked Margaret.

"I said I'm unhappy."

I wonder whether Margaret ever paid attention to what Carl thought or felt. Some people have thought processes that occupy their minds most of the time, which makes it difficult to hear what others are saying to them. It's as if they were listening to an internal dialogue instead of to the person who is talking to them. I thought that perhaps Margaret was one of these people.

"I am guilty," continued Margaret. "A lot of the problem is my responsibility. I bring things up that go way back. We've been married thirty-one years, and I have these old resentments that I just can't forget. A big one is that when I met him he was a married man. I dated him for a year not knowing that he was married. He didn't tell me the truth. He finally told me when his divorce came through, just a few weeks before we got married."

Old Resentments

Margaret's problem is typical of those people who simply cannot let go of the past. She had been married to Carl for more than thirty years. They had raised two daughters who were now adults. Yet she was still upset about her husband's behavior when she first met him, more than thirty-one years ago. Their past was very much a part of her present.

I suspected that Carl had never been able to recover the trust that he'd violated during that first year of courtship. I guessed that even though he had been a good provider, a loyal husband, and a good father, Margaret was still suspicious of him. I wondered how this lack of trust affected the couple's financial situation in the present.

I repressed my curiosity, however, because I wanted Margaret to remember some good times before we discussed financial problems. Good memories are the best antidote to bad ones. It is best to talk about money problems in the context of mutual affection rather than after discussing old resentments. So I asked Margaret, "Do you remember when he first swept you off your feet?"

I deliberately phrased the question so that it would have romantic and sexual connotations. I knew I was going to have to do something to revive the couple's attraction to one another, and I wanted to see whether there was a spark still there that could be lighted.

The Electric Arm

Margaret remembered that she had met Carl at a dance. "A school-teacher friend of mine introduced us when I arrived," she said. "He said, 'Have we met before?' I said, 'I was wondering the same thing.'

He looked pretty good to me, and my blind date hadn't shown up. So we talked, and it turned out that we had mutual friends."

"You really have a good memory," I said. Turning to the husband I added, "Has she always been able to remember this well?"

"All the details," said Carl.

"That's wonderful," I said.

"But not for the relationship," said Margaret, "because I go back . . ."

"Was that the night when he swept you off your feet?" I interrupted.

Margaret resumed her story. "When I finally convinced him that I couldn't go out with him that night because of my girlfriend, he just put his arm around me, and it was an electric arm." She laughed, and Carl smiled affectionately. "That was when I knew," said Margaret. "I had dated other guys before, but I never felt that, whatever it was, when he just put his arm around me. And then he said [she made a deep voice], 'I'll see you tomorrow then.'"

I felt that I had succeeded in bringing back a fond memory. I knew that there was a spark there of the old passion that had brought Margaret and Carl together. Yet the good memory was fleeting. Margaret went on.

"But then I didn't know all the other stuff. When I found out that I'd been with a married man, it did something to me that has been with me all these years. I would like to put this stuff behind me. A friend suggested that when I start thinking about it I should try meditation. But it doesn't work. I can't concentrate."

Retirement Money

Margaret went on to talk about more recent problems. "Carl retired in April," she said. "There's this document that the spouse has to sign, the annuity in a lump sum. I told him I wouldn't sign. I said that if we divorce I want the house, a car, and an amount of money in cash. Those are the conditions for me to sign. So I'm holding out to see where we're at."

Carl had held a government job for most of his working life. Now he couldn't withdraw his retirement money because Margaret refused to sign. I could see that this was a tense situation and imagined that Carl must feel humiliated and embarrassed because his wife was putting him through this ordeal.

Margaret continued, "If we decide not to divorce, then naturally I would go ahead and sign. But then I don't want him to hold it against me that I didn't sign before. I hope that he won't hold a grudge against me and that we can have a good relationship. If we stay together it should be nice between us."

Margaret couldn't let go of her resentments, but she didn't want Carl to hold any grudges. The part of her that lived in the past was expecting a divorce, so she was blackmailing her husband by refusing to sign his annuity. The part of her that lived in the present knew that they could stay together and be happy. I had to find a way to block the past and help her live in the present.

"We don't communicate at home," Margaret went on. "Each one goes his own way and does his own thing. We just need a better relationship." She turned to her husband, "Don't you agree?"

"Absolutely," said Carl.

I asked him what changes he would like to see in the relationship.

"A number of things," he said. "She just mentioned a few things that she has not left behind. But she never leaves *anything* behind. She has been threatening divorce over twenty, twenty-five years."

The person who threatens divorce holds all the power in a marriage. By questioning the very existence of the relationship, all aspects of marital life are at risk. The very threat of divorce denies the commitment of the spouses and threatens the whole institution of the family. I had to help Margaret to overcome her resentments and stop threatening Carl with divorce.

"So this isn't something that has come up in the last few weeks?" I asked.

"No," said Carl. "She's even told the kids many times that the marriage is going to end. Another major problem is that I'm a fairly active person. I'm always doing things. But she doesn't want to participate in social or civic events. She just likes to come home from work and go to bed."

I guessed that Carl and Margaret not only did not share a social life but also did not have a sex life. They presented the typical problems of middle-aged and older couples: old resentments, a mediocre sex life, and an emotional divorce that interfered with the possibility of enjoying each other. My job was to change all this. I decided to start with the old resentments.

The Statute of Limitations

"I would like to address three issues," I said. "The first is that even for the worst criminal there is a statute of limitations, and it is seven years. The law of this country is that a person cannot be tried for a crime that was committed more than seven years in the past. I want the same law to apply to your marriage. So I want you to focus on your resentments but only of the last seven years."

Margaret's response was predictable. "The last seven years haven't been too stormy," she said. She didn't want to focus on problems because I asked her to do it.

I turned to Carl, "Are you willing to do that?"

"I always forget about our disagreements," said Carl. "I'm more than willing to do that!" he laughed.

Margaret continued, "Why can't we just say that we'd like to get a fresh start, wipe the slate clean, make every day the beginning of a new relationship?"

"Wait, I can't believe this," said Carl. "Is that what you want to do?"

"I do," said Margaret. "But it's something that we both have to do. Not just me—you too."

"If that's what you want to do, that's fine," I said. "But for this therapy you have permission to go seven years. And that applies to both of you."

"I'll be delighted," said Carl laughing.

"OK," said Margaret, "so if I want to say something I have to remember whether it was beyond seven years and not talk about it?"

"Carl's job will be to remind you," I said.

"And I will remind him," said Margaret.

"OK," I said, "so you think you can go no more than seven years in the past between now and next week?"

"Yes," said Margaret emphatically.

Money Secrets

My next step was to do something about Carl's retirement. As long as Margaret didn't sign, she was humiliating him in ways that were incompatible with a good relationship. I suspected that Margaret had secrets about her own finances and decided to act on that hunch.

I said, "I think we need to devote one entire session just to work out the finances."

Predictably, Margaret objected. "Why? I don't see that," she said. She didn't want to divulge what she did with the money that she made as an art teacher.

I said, "Both of you want to do the right thing by each other regarding your finances. The best way to do that is to bring everything together, sit down, and see what you have to work with."

Carl said, "I have long since given up any claims on her income. It bothered me for a while, but the bigger problem is that to receive my annuity she has to sign by Friday."

Margaret ignored Carl's statement and, turning to me, said, "Right now I have too many outstanding bills from my credit cards in department stores," which was exactly what I suspected.

"Would you be willing to bring all that information here?" I asked. "I want to devote one session to figuring out what you've got."

Carl said, "If we don't do something about my annuity by Friday, it's cause for additional . . ."

Margaret interrupted him, "I'm going to sign it, OK?"

"Say that again?" said Carl.

"I said I'm going to sign it. I see that you're sincere about improving our relationship."

Carl looked at her, his mouth open with astonishment and happiness.

I said, "I'd like you to get up and give your wife a hug and thank her for that."

Carl stood up, bent over to his wife, and embraced her, kissing her tenderly.

Margaret said, "Now I don't want you to hold a grudge against me and tell me what I put you through."

Carl agreed more than happily.

"What's Mine Is Mine and What's Yours Is Mine Also"

In every marriage there are tacit contracts about money. Even though a couple may never discuss explicitly how money will be handled, rules develop, patterns are established, and change becomes difficult if not impossible.

The most stable couples are those who have a complementary relationship. The spouses complement each other in the way they handle money, which means that different rules apply to the way husband and wife are to handle their finances. They are not equal.

For example, a traditional complementary relationship is one where the husband works, brings home a paycheck, and hands it over to his wife. She manages the home and the children and pays the bills, deciding how money will be spent. In this way, each spouse has different areas of responsibility, and each has power over different aspects of life. He has power as a breadwinner and provider; she has power over spending and family relationships. Each depends on the other, and so the relationship will tend to be stable.

The fact that a relationship is stable, however, doesn't mean that it is satisfactory. Husband and wife may be unhappy together, but they may not be able to separate because they complement each other, need each other. Carl and Margaret were in a stable, unsatisfactory relationship. They complemented each other in a special way. They both worked and made money. In that sense they had a symmetrical relationship, but they were complementary in that Carl gave Margaret the money he made and so provided for the home and the family. Margaret kept the money that she made to herself and spent it on herself. Margaret's money belonged only to her, and Carl's money belonged only to Margaret.

The marriage had destabilized when Margaret refused to sign for Carl's annuity. To Carl, this was the last straw. He was willing to give her everything, but he wanted to have a say over his retirement money. When Margaret promised to sign, the couple was ready to go back to their previous, complementary way of dealing with each other. My problem was how to help them have a happier relationship without necessarily changing the rules about how they handled money. I believe that a therapist must be careful not to change that which a couple has not requested help in changing.

Turning on the Electricity

I told Margaret that I wanted to speak to Carl alone for a few minutes and asked her to go to the waiting room. Then I said to Carl, "I think she needs to feel your electric arm again. When you told me a few minutes ago that when she comes home she goes straight to bed, I was thinking that maybe she's giving you the message that she wants you to join her."

"I don't know," said Carl. "She complains about the absence of sex, but when I want to have sex with her she says she doesn't want it."

I insisted, "Yet I think that she still has an expectation of that electric arm that she talked about, that electricity that your arm was able to incite in her. Would you be willing to turn on her electricity again?"

"I can try, but she says, 'I can't have sex with you; it's been so long, I'm sure you must be getting it some place, and there's AIDS and all this other stuff.'"

"I know there is a passion that need to be reestablished," I said. "I can see that it's there. It's just dormant right now."

I realized that Carl, by himself, would not be able to revive the passion so I decided next to see Margaret alone and try to influence her. I started by asking her how she thought the love between her and her husband could be revived.

She said, "I'm going to be very personal here for a moment. It's been almost three years since there's been a sexual relationship between us. I don't have any proof that he's been involved with another woman although there were times I suspected it. I don't believe a man is going to go for two years without sex. Whether he has or not, I don't know. And now so much time has gone by that I don't want AIDS or something. So I'll never be able to have sex again."

"Look," I said, "I'm worried because I can see that you chose a great husband who has been supportive of you in so many ways, financially, emotionally, with the children. He has been a protector, a provider. All of a sudden you are going to walk right out the door, and some other woman, not nearly as deserving as yourself, is going to snatch him."

"Some friends said that to me," she said.

"The problem for you is how to bring back that affection, that desire, the way he put that arm . . ."

Margaret interrupted me, "Maybe I could cook something that he likes. Right now I never cook for him."

"What would you cook for a very romantic evening?"

"He's not fastidious—anything that's food, you know."

"So would you put candles on the table?"

"I could, but I never have."

"Would you do it this week?"

"Well, I don't know. Our relationship is based on money, not love. If I don't sign the annuity, he's going to want a divorce."

"I have no doubt that he loves you," I said.

"You think so? How do you know?"

"A therapist knows. And I think it would shatter him if you walked out. I don't think you would be able to pick up the pieces. He needs to come home to a surprise, a candlelight dinner. Would you know how to seduce him?"

"I probably could," said Margaret. "But what's in it for me?"

"You need what is waiting from all that. . . ."

Margaret laughed.

"Which is him and his electricity again," I continued.

"His electricity is not there," she said.

"I think you can use your charms to arouse that arm again. Which night are you going to do it?"

"Wait a minute. I don't even know if he has AIDS. I could have him get checked, but it would take a while. Why would I do all this if I don't want it to go but so far?"

"That's a very good point. What you could do is go to the drugstore and do what women of a younger generation would do. Buy three or four different-colored condoms, and ask him to pick a color."

Margaret laughed. "I think I'd be embarrassed."

"You want to do it to arouse that electricity."

Margaret laughed again, embarrassed.

"Perhaps you could ask one of your daughters to buy the condoms, because this is something a young woman would do without any embarrassment."

"I could ask the one that is married," said Margaret.

"Then, after the candlelight dinner, ask your husband to pick a color. It'll be fun."

"He's going to say, 'You have some nerve!' It's been a long time now. He might have a medical problem. Several years ago I saw a medical bill that said something about a prostrate problem. Of course, it did say, 'Does not affect ability to function.'"

"Well, no matter what happens, you can have fun that night. Do you have a negligée?"

"Yes."

"Can you have all this as a surprise for him?"

"It can be done. All I have to do is go to the store and get something to cook, set the table, light the candles, and put the negligée on. It won't be so much of an ordeal."

"OK," I said, "I'll see you next week."

A Fresh Start

When they came to the next session, Margaret said, "This past week has been wonderful. We talked. This is too good to be true."

Carl agreed.

Margaret laughed as she recalled how the previous night, when she had the candlelight dinner ready, Carl had walked into the house and said, "Am I in the right house? Is this the Margaret that I know?" She laughed.

Most couples who have been together many years face the problem of how to recover their attraction to one another and their sexual interest. Carl and Margaret were able to do it in three steps:

1. They compromised over money issues. Margaret signed for the annuity, and Carl did not intrude on her secrets about how she spent her money.

2. They agreed on the statute of limitations and therefore eliminated about twenty-five years of past resentments.

3. Margaret successfully seduced Carl back into a sexual relationship.

Steps to Improve an Older Couple's Relationship

Typical problems of middle-aged or older couples are old resentments, a mediocre sex life, unfair financial arrangements, a tiresome social life, and what often appears to be an emotional divorce.

There are several steps that a couple or one of the spouses can follow to bring changes in these areas. These steps are quite different from those for younger couples.

Lighting the Fire

The first step is for a couple to recover some of the passion they had for one another in the past. Certain conversations are helpful in this regard. You can talk about how you met, what attracted each to the other, what "swept you off your feet," how you fell in love. Just to talk about this sometimes brings back a spark of the old feelings.

As you talk, you need to pay attention to your words to pick up on phrases or expressions that reflect attraction and passion and that later can be used as triggers to bring back those feelings. For example, a woman told her husband that the first time he embraced her he felt like a big warm teddy bear. He remembered those words and used them repeatedly to remind her of their love, saying for instance, 'I think you need to cuddle with your teddy bear.' The teddy bear became the metaphor for the love and passion they had for one another.

The Statute of Limitations

You and your spouse can handle old resentments by using the concept of the statute of limitations. When applied to marriage, this means that you cannot bring up, allude to, or express resentments or accusations about things that happened more than seven years ago. This includes misuse of funds, affairs, betrayal, or whatever. It is important to focus on the problems of the last seven years but to set aside those that happened previously.

Should one spouse forget the rule about the statute of limitations when talking about the past, the other can point out that you cannot talk about that. This forces each of you to make the effort of remembering what year you are talking about every time you begin to express old resentments, which can become quite tedious and a deterrent to expressing old resentments.

When you have been married for twenty or thirty years, many old resentments can be remembered to throw a damper on attempts to come closer together. The limit of seven years makes for a more manageable time frame. It is also better than trying to forget all the past and only focusing on the present and the future, which most couples find too extreme. In fact, what often happens is that as a couple makes the effort to remember that they cannot talk about complaints that are more than seven years old, they conclude that it would be easier to have a fresh start and forget the whole past.

Financial Planning

Every couple needs to have a financial plan. You have to organize your finances as best you can in a fair way. This approach is similar to what young couples also need to do, but it is even more necessary since the financial problems of older people are usually more complicated.

It is difficult to succeed at marital happiness when there are unresolved financial issues that make you resentful of one another. You and your spouse need to have a common ideology in marriage, a shared vision of what it is that you are struggling for, what you want to accomplish as a couple and as a family. This ideology always includes issues about wants and needs in the material realm.

Reviving Your Sex Life

Once financial problems are resolved so at least there is agreement and collaboration, you can begin to revive your sex life. You need to experiment with approaching one another in unusual, fun ways. You can welcome your spouse at the door wearing nothing but a kitchen apron. You might invite your spouse to a hotel where you can both have a jacuzzi bath together. Each of you can respond to the other's objections and reluctance and deal with your own fear of rejection in playful ways and by remembering the trust and love that you once had for one another. Remember all that you have invested in your spouse over the years, and don't lose that investment.

Accounting for the Last Seven Years

Reevaluate the last seven years of life together (remembering the statute of limitations). Think about what is the worst thing that each of you has done to the other. Then evaluate, using common sense, as to how bad things really are. If you have really hurt one another, it's important to recognize this and put it in the context of good things you have also done. You may be harboring resentments over truly ridiculous things, however, and it's also important to recognize this. Each of you can think of what other husbands and wives have been known to do to each other and make a comparison with your own situation, taking the opportunity to congratulate yourselves on the minimal ways in which you have hurt each other.

The Future

Talk about your future plans, fun times, vacations, perhaps a second honeymoon. Promise one another that the threat of divorce is abandoned once and for all. You cannot have fun together when one of you is threatening with divorce.

To summarize, remember that inside you is a core of the love and passion that you've had for one another and that you will carry into the future. Remember that the expression of resentments on either one's part is truly a request for love. The appropriate response to resentment is love, much as young couples respond to provocation with humor and play instead of hostility. Older couples need to respond to resentments with love instead of with anger or withdrawal. Plan your finances carefully and fairly, and share a vision of what you would like your financial situation to be like. Give up old grudges about how money was handled in the past. Don't use money to threaten one another. When money becomes the bond that holds a couple together, the bond of love is weakened and destroyed.

Money can sometimes create long-lasting resentments, but it can also be used in positive ways. In the next chapter, we will discuss some unusual ways in which money can help you overcome difficult problems.

Chapter Ten

The Positive Use of Money

Most of us are bothered at one time or another by something we can't stop doing. Perhaps we smoke, eat too much, don't exercise, or procrastinate in our work. If this is your situation, you can use money to change these behaviors.

Sometimes we are bothered by the behavior of those we love. These behaviors may be self-destructive or destructive to their relationship with us. When you're tired of pleading with your husband, begging your children, negotiating with your wife, think about the possibility of "an offer that they can't refuse."[1]

We have seen how money can have strings attached that are destructive. But money can also have strings attached that are constructive. You can use it to help yourself or others overcome difficult problems. When those you love are engaging in destructive behaviors, you can link their personality traits to their unwanted behaviors so they will change. The link is money.

Money Tricks

It would be nice if people would change and do what is best for them because they have insight into their behavior or because they love us. But this is often not the case. Change is difficult, but it can be made a little easier by using money wisely and strategically. We all want to lead a balanced life, yet our lives often become unbalanced. Money can give that little extra weight that tips the scale so that we're balanced again.

Collecting Fines

Imposing fines on family members for certain behaviors is useful when people are not doing what they are supposed to do. Often, parents impose fines on children for not doing their chores, receiving unsatisfactory grades, or fighting with each other. It is more unusual for a spouse to impose a fine on another spouse. But it is possible.

My friend Betty's husband, Joe, had a heart condition. He needed to exercise regularly and had to avoid certain foods. Betty reminded him every day about exercising, was careful not to buy any fattening foods, and begged him to take care of himself. But Joe hated to exercise. He loved good food and restaurants. He specially enjoyed creamy, sugary things. Joe claimed that he had a chronic state of anxiety, for some mysterious biological reason, that prevented him from resisting the temptation of eating cookies and other goodies and interfered with his will power to exercise.

Betty was tired of nagging him and worrying. She threatened and cajoled him to no avail. She threatened to leave him, but even this threat didn't move him to change.

One day, Betty decided to try a new tactic. She invited Joe to a fancy restaurant and as they were eating his favorite food, she said she had something to propose to him that would make her very happy. In fact, if he accepted it, she would be so happy that she would never nag him again about exercising or dieting.

Joe was curious, especially about the idea that she would stop nagging. He begged her to explain the proposition.

"I've come to realize, Joe," said Betty, "that you have the right to do as you please with your life, particularly when you live in such a state of anxiety. No one should tell you how to live and what to do." Joe couldn't believe his ears.

"Yet," Betty continued, "your behavior makes me very sad. I feel that if it continues, I'll have to prepare for becoming a widow in the very near future. I'm very anxious about this, and I need your help to calm my anxiety."

"I'll certainly try to help you," said Joe, "but what's your proposition?"

Betty went on to say Joe knew how she liked to have money and buy pretty things for herself and their daughters.

"In fact," said Betty, "money is a great tranquilizer for my anxiety."

"I know that," said Joe.

"And you just promised to help me with my anxiety," Betty reminded him.

So, Betty told Joe that every time that he ate outside his diet, she wanted him to pay her a certain amount of money, for her to do with as she pleased. "So let's talk about how much each treat will cost you."

Joe was astounded. After a long negotiation, they agreed that for each cookie that he ate, he would pay her $1; a tablespoon of butter was worth $2; a piece of meat was worth $5; anything with caffeine, $2.50; and so on. And for any day he didn't do his twenty minutes on the treadmill, he had to pay her $20.

Betty looked dreamy as she talked about the clothes she would buy with all the money she would be making. "I was considering divorce very seriously," said Betty, "but I think this is better."

"You were really going to leave me?" asked Joe.

"Yes," said Betty. "I couldn't tolerate the anxiety of watching you eat yourself to death. But I guess everybody has a price, and the money will reassure me."

"You won't have to leave me, and I won't have to pay you," said Joe, "because I won't eat any of those things."

Yet, in the next few weeks, Joe had to pay. He skipped exercise one day and ate a box of cookies on another occasion. Betty was very strict about collecting her fee. Soon, however, Joe began to think twice before committing a misdemeanor. He began to eat properly and was eventually on his way to a healthier lifestyle.

Charging Fees

Gordon and Joyce had been to therapists for years because of their marital problems. They were both successful professionals who came from very different backgrounds. He was Jewish from New York, and she was Protestant from a small town in England. They had been stormily married for more than twenty years. I was the last therapist they were going to try. If I failed to reconcile their differences, they would finally divorce.

Joyce and Gordon could not have been more different from one another. He loved parties; she hated them. He wanted to travel; she wanted to stay home. He wanted spontaneity; she needed careful planning. Gordon worked long hours and was frequently away on business trips. Joyce's work as a consultant kept her at home most of the time.

"What I most resent about Gordon," said Joyce, "are certain idiosyncracies that I can't understand or forgive. For example, he's always late for everything."

"She always has to be early for everything," interjected Gordon.

I had noticed that Joyce arrived twenty minutes early to our appointment and Gordon was ten minutes late.

"If I expect him to come home for dinner," continued Joyce, "he will inevitably arrive at least half an hour late. He's also always late when he has to meet me at a restaurant, the movies, at a party, or in the street."

Over the years, Joyce had felt more and more desperately out of control, at Gordon's mercy, and repeatedly threatened divorce. Gordon was upset about his own tardiness but said he was helpless to change.

Joyce was about to continue with another complaint, when I interrupted her. "I'd like to start with the problem of punctuality first," I said.

"You have to understand," Gordon interrupted, "that my work is often unpredictable. I am often delayed by meetings and urgent phone calls," he said. "I can't be punctual."

"We'll see about that," I answered. "I think I have a solution if you do as I say."

Reluctantly, he agreed.

I told him that every time he was late and his wife was waiting for him at home, he would pay her $1 for every minute he was late.

If she was waiting at someone else's home, a restaurant, and such, he would pay her $2 for every minute he was late. If she was out in the street, the price would be $3 per minute. And if it was raining, the weather was cold, or it was snowing, the fine would be $5 per minute. He would always have to carry cash, because the payment would be in cash at the time he was late—no checks or delayed payments.

As for Joyce, the money that she made on his tardiness, she could only spend on herself, not on the house or children. She loved the idea.

From then on, Joyce never again complained to me about Gordon's lack of punctuality. When he was late, he paid her every time, and I suspect that she began to encourage his tardiness. In fact, I never knew whether he became more punctual or whether punctuality just stopped being an issue.

Once this problem was taken care of, I moved on to another conflict. Gordon's profession entailed an active social life. He had to take people out to dinner and attend parties and other events. Joyce hated his social life. She would usually refuse to participate in events involving his colleagues, and if she attended, she was often disagreeable. He felt mistreated and was disappointed because he admired her intelligence and wanted to show off his wife. They had bitter, violent fights about this problem.

"How much do you charge as a consultant?" I asked Joyce. "Do you charge by the hour?"

"Yes," answered Joyce, "$60 an hour."

"Gordon," I said, "I think you can solve this problem. And I understand how important it is for you, how much you want Joyce's company. This is what I propose. Every time you want your wife's company at a social event, you should pay her her hourly fee to attend." Gordon looked at me with amazement. "Minus a small discount," I added, "because, after all, you're her husband. I think $50 the hour would be fair." Joyce was looking at me with interest. "So if she has to go to a dinner," I continued, "a party, or any other social occasion where you want her presence, you will pay her $50 for every hour she's there."

I turned to Joyce. "Now, since you're being paid as a professional," I explained, "you will have to behave as such. You will be polite and interested in the people you meet. You'll go out of your way to engage them in interesting conversations. You will treat everyone with the same consideration you show when you're working as a consultant."

"Does travel time count?" asked Joyce, surprising me with the question. Obviously, she liked the idea. "Some of his functions are an hour's drive away. I should be paid for sitting in the car."

"I don't have that much money," complained Gordon. "Already I'm paying her for being late. Now, I'm going to have to pay her to come to dinner. I'm going to go bankrupt."

"I don't think so," I answered. "I think it's a fair arrangement. You're the one that needs Joyce's presence. I think that $30 for travel time would be fair."

Joyce agreed, and Gordon accepted. From then on, the couple's social life was no longer a problem, although once in a while Gordon would mutter something under his breath about all I was costing him.

Preventing Sabotage

Neil was the therapist of a twelve-year-old boy, Josh, who was verbally abusive toward his mother. He met with the parents and tried to organize them to stop this behavior with rules for Josh about appropriate language and consequences if the rules were disobeyed. But the parents did not follow through by enforcing the rules and consequences.

Neil could see that the father sabotaged every effort to control the boy. He suspected that Josh was talking for the father and expressing the father's anger by insulting the mother. Yet the problem had to be solved, or the boy would become more and more disturbed and the mother more and more angry.

Neil told the father that he wanted him to do only one thing. Every time Josh insulted his mother, the father was to give him $1, since the boy was under his employment. No other explanation was given. The father was mortified, but the insults ended.

Avoiding Procrastination

Marie came to therapy because she had a serious problem about writing her dissertation. She was working on her Ph.D. for a European university but found all kinds of excuses to write things other than her thesis. This tactic wasn't difficult to do because she worked as a journalist. I sympathized with her problem and asked her about her family, friends, life in Europe, how she got along with her siblings.

Marie said that she had a stepsister in Europe whom she disliked intensely. I changed the subject of conversation back to her dissertation and asked how many pages a day she could reasonably expect to write. She said four.

I told Marie there was a solution to her problem, which she probably wouldn't like, but she knew how important it was to finish her Ph.D.

I said, "Every day that you don't write four pages, I want you to write a $50 check to your sister and mail it to her with a note saying, 'With all my love' or 'Thinking about you!'"

Marie said this was the last thing she wanted to do and immediately began to negotiate exceptions. I agreed that if there were an international crisis and she had to fly somewhere to report it, that would not count. She was not expected to write on the airplane or while reporting.

The dissertation was finished in a few months, and the sister never got a check.

Giving money to people you love is a way of helping you change. An even more effective way is to give money to people you dislike.

Avoiding Anxiety

Some people are plagued by feelings of anxiety that they can't get rid of. The anxiety appears for no apparent reason and doesn't go away. It can prevent us from enjoying our work, family, and social life. Giving money to people one dislikes is not only a way of avoiding procrastination—it's a way of preventing anxiety.

Ralph had always been hard-working, and he had succeeded. He had a good job, a beautiful wife, and two wonderful children. Yet he was plagued by a strange anxiety that would overcome him unexpectedly. At business meetings, while driving to work, even at school parties for his children, the anxiety would creep into him and disturb him. He was so upset by it that just talking to me made him worry that the feeling would come back.

I asked him about his family, friends, work. We talked about the people he loved and the ones he disliked. I asked him who was the person he disliked the most.

"It's got to be my brother-in-law," said Ralph. "I think he's a creep. He doesn't take work seriously, he's not a good provider, and he's not nice to my sister."

"What kind of relationship do you have with him?" I asked.

"Not very good," he said. "I basically avoid him."

"Do you think your sister would like for you to be friends?"

"Probably," he said, "but I can't stand him."

"Good," I said. "You need a consequence for your anxiety, one that is negative enough that it'll discourage you from being anxious. Every time you feel abnormally anxious, I want you to send your brother-in-law a gift with a card saying how much you appreciate him."

"He's going to think I want to be friends!" exclaimed Ralph. "Besides, I don't have money to waste on him!"

"Exactly," I said. "If you don't want to waste your money on him, just stop feeling anxious."

After a few presents to his brother-in-law, Ralph's anxiety diminished and soon disappeared.

Preventing Wife Abuse

Husbands who abuse their wives typically argue that they can't control their behavior.

Sally and Bruno came to see me as the last resort. Sally had said that if the therapy didn't work and Bruno hit her one more time, she would press charges against him. Bruno, ashamed of his behavior, argued that Sally provoked it.

I explained that the law punishes violence, not provocation, and that the judge would not be sympathetic to the argument that Sally was provocative. I said I wanted to help Bruno remain a law-abiding citizen and a productive member of the community.

I proposed the following. Bruno was to open a bank account in the name of his mother-in-law. In that account he would deposit $200. Should he hit his wife again, the money would automatically go to the mother-in-law, and he would have to deposit another $200 in the account. That is, each blow to his wife would cost him $200.

Since it was possible that Sally would provoke Bruno to hit her, given that her mother was poor and needed the money, I suggested the following. If Bruno thought that he had hit Sally because she provoked him, then the money, instead of going to her mother, would go to a charity. In any case, he would lose $200. I added that if the violence stopped, I would teach both of them how to negotiate peacefully.

Bruno never hit his wife again, and they eventually learned to communicate with one another.

Preventing Self-Deprecation

Pauline was an attractive, successful executive—a self-made woman who appeared strong and competent yet was plagued with feelings of insecurity and doubts about herself. She had spent years in therapy talking about her low self-esteem, which she attributed to the fact that as a child her mother used to beat her.

She had been rejected by her first husband and eventually married a second time to a middle-aged bachelor. The husband soon lost his job at the beginning of the 1990s recession and refused to look for another job. He also refused to have sex with Pauline, even though once in a while he would show her how he could still have an erection.

Pauline attributed her poor choice of husbands to her low self-esteem. When she consulted me, I first tried to convince her about what was obvious: she was intelligent, beautiful, successful, powerful, and she made a lot of money. She countered that none of this meant anything to her. She was just an abused woman with low self-esteem. She told me about how she frequently fought with her husband and how they would push each other, pull each other's hair, and verbally abuse one another. He was a big man, so she was the one who would usually get hurt.

"Pauline," I said, "why do you stay with this man? He is abusive, he doesn't give you sex, and he doesn't even try to find a job. Have you considered that perhaps you'd be better off without him?"

"I know," she said, "but I can't leave him. I'm too insecure; I feel worthless."

So I helped Pauline avoid fighting with her husband, and the verbal and physical abuse stopped. But he still wouldn't have sex with her, and he still wouldn't go to work. And Pauline still kept talking about how she was an abused woman with low self-esteem. In the meantime, her accomplishments at work increased, and she was promoted.

Finally, one day I said to Pauline, "I'm tired of listening to your absurd complaints about abuse and low self-esteem. They are totally contradictory with any sense of reality about who you are. I want you to meditate about what it is to truly be an abused woman. If you understand that, you'll stop having these ridiculous thoughts. So what I want you to do is that every time the thought that you are an abused or worthless woman crosses your mind for more than thirty seconds, I want you to write a check for $100 to a shelter for abused women and mail it immediately. If the thought crosses your mind a second time, the check will be for $150, and so on. Your negative thoughts will cost you so much money that hopefully you'll want to make a serious effort to get rid of them. Yet if you don't, at least some good will result: women who are truly abused will be helped."

Pauline began to send checks to the House of Ruth. She sent so much money, she didn't even want to tell me how much. Then one day I began to notice that we were no longer talking about her low self-esteem. She surprised me by reporting that she had moved out of her house and separated from her husband.

Most of us try to be cautious about how we use our money. We don't want to overspend or overpay. Yet, sometimes money can be used in ways that seem wasteful but can stop unwanted behaviors that are emotionally very costly. Money can be a balancing force in our lives.

The next chapter deals with the problems of families when money is used irrationally for secret and hidden reasons.

Chapter Eleven

Money and Irrational Behavior

We all struggle with the issue of sharing power in the family. This power not only involves who makes decisions for others and who has control but also who takes care of whom and who protects whom.

We all go through stages in family life when power issues predominate. One is adolescence and young adulthood, a time when young people begin to take control of their lives and may clash with the parents' authority. The other is the marital relationship, which changes over the years so that control and responsibilities have to be renegotiated.

Money is power, and the struggle for power often involves a struggle to control the money in the family. Control over money can be obtained in three different ways: through negotiation, seduction, and irrational behavior. In negotiating, people do what you want because you have convinced them that it's best. In seduction, people do what you want because they love you and want to please you. Most of the time, we negotiate and seduce in our relationships with our loved ones.

Yet, sometimes we can feel so powerless that we resort to irrational behavior. When we feel that we are treated unjustly and when negotiations and seduction fail, we can be prone to becoming irrational. There is a terrorist lurking inside all of us, ready to come out when negotiations have failed and we are losing.

When we are resentful, we can behave irrationally in ways that cause financial damage to the family. If we have access to family money, the irrational behavior may be associated with overspending or secret spending (such as gambling or running up credit cards) or refusing to work and make money. If we do not have direct access to family money, the irrational behavior may be associated with running up bills that the family has to pay, such as medical treatments or having to be bailed out of jail. In the first case, we

spend money directly. In the second case, we make the family
spend money because of us.

Couples

Spouses divide responsibilities in many different ways. With one
couple, for example, the wife makes all the decisions having to do
with home and children, while the husband makes all the decisions
about money and social life. With another couple, the wife makes
all the decisions about money, while the husband makes all the
decisions about family and friends.

Whichever way responsibilities are divided, every couple has
to deal with two main issues: providing and spending. In some
couples, both husband and wife contribute to providing and
spending. Both have to negotiate how much each provides to
the common pot and what power each has to spend. In other
couples, one provides, and the other spends. Sometimes, only
one of the spouses provides, and only that spouse decides on how
to spend.

Issues around providing and spending can lead to conflicts and
struggles that remain unresolved. One of the spouses may feel
powerless in the relationship and attempt to resolve the struggle by
deriving power from irrational behavior.

Irrational behavior by a family member undermines the family
structure, not only because it is disturbing to everyone but because
it affects the whole family's ability to function and therefore always
results in financial loss. This attack can be active or passive. *Active*

When the attack is active, typical irrational behaviors are over-
spending, gambling, and stealing. When the attack is passive, irra- *pas*
tional behaviors are refusal to work, physical illness, depression,
compulsions, anxiety, panic, eating disorders, drug addiction, and
alcoholism. All these irrational behaviors are costly but desperate
attempts to balance power in the marriage.

Gambling

Dora and Alex couldn't agree on nearly anything. Every time they talked, they quarreled. Alex felt that during the week, when he had to work, Dora was unsupportive and bitchy. Unable to change Dora's behavior, Alex countered by spending the weekends placing bets on football games over the phone. He wanted to have more power in the marriage, and he thought that by engaging in gambling, which Dora couldn't control, he would gain that power. Instead, he only strained the family finances and increased the marital unhappiness.

Dora suffered long hours watching Alex compromise the family future, which only increased her resentment and bitchiness. Eventually Alex realized that gambling was an irrational behavior that didn't give him more power in the marriage. It simply undermined the family finances and created new difficulties. He decided he had to change or lose his marriage. He became extremely considerate to Dora, calling her from work every day to see how she was doing and asking if he could help when she was in a bad mood. During the weekends, he stopped gambling and played with the children instead.

At first Dora couldn't believe how Alex had changed. She was suspicious and afraid to expect that the change would last. But after a few weeks, she too changed and they were able to recover the good relationship they had had during their courtship.

Overspending

Diane was tired of Doug's stonewalling. His passivity infuriated her. His withdrawal and sarcasm made her feel unappreciated. Diane was temperamental and prone to rages when she would scream and break things. Later she felt like a fool.

After several years of marriage, Diane decided to increase her power through more effective means than raging. Every time they quarreled and Doug became withdrawn or sarcastic, Diane went shopping. She would buy a piece of jewelry, charging it to Doug's credit card, and come home cheerful. As soon as she saw Doug, she would thank him effusively and show him the present he had just bought for her to make up for their quarrel.

Diane got even with Doug without raging, but her method undermined the family finances. Doug worried about the money and wanted to change Diane's behavior. He began to stop her every time she was walking out the door after a quarrel. Each time he would apologize, even though it was difficult for him to do so, and asked Diane to go out with him instead of by herself. Soon he began to succeed in obtaining her forgiveness, and after some time they stopped quarreling so frequently.

Procrastinating

Eddie and Debbie were happily married for many years. He was an accountant who worked hard to support the family. Debbie stayed home and took care of the children. When the youngest child left for college, Debbie decided to go back to school. She became a psychologist and started a practice.

As Debbie began to work, she had less time for Eddie. She had to work evening hours so he often had dinner alone. He attempted many times to negotiate Debbie's hours so she would work less in the evening. But she refused to change her schedule or spend more time with him, saying that her career came first. They had a weekend house that they both had loved, but she claimed to be too busy to go with him there.

Feeling neglected, Eddie began to procrastinate at work. He didn't pay his own taxes, and he began to lose clients because he was so late in paying theirs. The family finances suffered. Debbie became very worried about the increasing amounts owed to the IRS, since now they had to not only pay their taxes but also fines.

Debbie began to suspect that Eddie's procrastination was a reaction to her increasing success and withdrawal. Since Eddie failed to engage Debbie by explicitly asking for her attention, he had resorted to covert means. His procrastination had succeeded in getting Debbie's attention, but at the cost of serious financial difficulties.

Debbie realized that, although she constantly worried about her husband and offered support and advice, she failed to change him. She had become more and more exasperated, since their financial situation was seriously jeopardized by his refusal to do his work. After many attempts to coax, encourage, and support him, she decided to change her approach.

Debbie gave her husband a schedule with deadlines for him to fulfill certain business obligations. If he did not meet them during a specified period of time, she would go to his office and do them herself, even though that would imply a considerable loss of money for the couple, since the husband was an expert and she was not.

Debbie began to call Eddie on the phone at his office regularly to make sure that he was working. She knew she had neglected him since she became involved in her career, so she decided to spend her evenings with him. She began to pursue him sexually.

Eddie responded well and began to do better in his work. The couple reached a new balance where both could be involved in their careers without competing with or neglecting each other. Debbie was able to change her behavior before serious damage had been done. She didn't sacrifice any of her power. On the contrary, she even threatened with taking charge of Eddie's work. But she listened to her husband's needs and reengaged with him so the marriage could continue in happiness. She was clever enough not to respond to Eddie's irrational behavior by behaving irrationally herself.

Stealing

Caroline was a beautiful model, afraid of aging. She feared she wouldn't be able to work when she grew older and also that her husband would leave her. Her husband, Bernard, kept stocks, bonds, money, and his family jewelry in a safe deposit box at a bank. He offered to keep the jewelry that he had given to Caroline in the same deposit box and gave her access to it. Bernard rarely used the box, but Caroline frequently took out her jewelry, then returned it for safekeeping.

One day Caroline and Bernard had a big argument about the risks he was taking in his business. Caroline thought that Bernard was acting irrationally but failed to convince him of her point of view.

Several days later, when Bernard went to the safe deposit box, he found it was empty. Caroline had taken everything he owned and refused to tell him where it was. She explained to Bernard that she needed to protect herself and plan for the future. Bernard cried and said he would leave her. TWO IRRATIONAL Behaviors

Caroline, thinking that Bernard was behaving irrationally in his business, responded with another irrational behavior: stealing. She thought that she would gain more power in the relationship. Yet she only accomplished an escalation, since now Bernard was threatening with leaving her.

The couple consulted with me and Caroline tearfully posed the problem of what to do now. I suggested that she apologize to Bernard for her irrational behavior. He in turn promised to discuss his business plans with her before taking any action. They left my office reconciled.

Overeating

Bob and Carol were a young couple with three children. Bob worked hard and made good money as an insurance salesman. He was the provider and also the one who decided how money should be spent. The couple had agreed that, even though Carol was a nurse, she would stay home and raise the children.

Over the years, Bob became more and more successful in his business but refused to improve the family's lifestyle. He invested every cent he made in real estate and wouldn't listen to Carol's demands for a little more comfort in the home. Carol was not a big spender, but she was tired of saving on food, their old car, and their shabby furniture.

Bob's refusal to negotiate about money actually made Carol sick to her stomach. Thinking that her nauseous feeling was hunger, she began to spend long, lonely hours, while the children were at school, eating everything that she could lay hands on. Sometimes she would go to the store and buy a whole cake that she would eat in one afternoon. Afraid of growing fat, she would then vomit. After vomiting, she would feel hungry again and start to eat once more. In order to buy the large quantities of food that she ate and vomited, Carol began to save on other expenses. Soon Bob noticed that he was never getting steak for dinner any more. Yet the grocery bills were getting higher and higher.

Finally, Carol confessed to what she was doing. The couple consulted a therapist who convinced Bob that he had to negotiate with Carol. When Carol gained more power over how money should be spent, she stopped bingeing and vomiting.

Getting Sick

The time when Ted would retire was approaching, so he started to plan where to live and how to finance the lifestyle that he wanted. Meanwhile, his wife Alice became upset when Ted refused to discuss any plans for the future with her.

After some time went by with bad feeling in the marriage, Alice began to obsess about cysts that she had noticed in her breasts. In spite of numerous tests, X rays, and sonograms that showed the cysts were benign, she insisted on an operation to remove them. The biopsies showed no signs of cancer, but she still stayed up all night, touching her breasts, looking for new cysts, certain that she had cancer. She began to use the family funds to travel to strange places looking for alternative medical approaches that would confirm her suspicions and offer a cure. Due to the medical and the travel expenses, Ted had to continue working and post-pone his retirement.

When Ted failed to negotiate, Alice became ill in such a way that both lost. Ted couldn't retire; Alice suffered operations; nei-ther could enjoy a better lifestyle.

After a couple of years, Ted once more had the possibility of retiring. This time he included Alice in his plans. After much negotiation, they compromised on a lifestyle that they both enjoyed and Ted was able to retire.

" MEN who won't change "

Compulsive Cleaning

Joan quit her job when she married her second husband, Alan. She thought she had worked enough in her life and would enjoy stay-ing home. She soon discovered, however, that she'd become totally dependent on Alan for money and entertainment. She wanted to go out to dinner and to take vacations. But Alan was much older than Joan and quite stingy. He wanted to stay at home and refused to negotiate any change in his habits.

Joan began to clean the house and everything in it—con-stantly and compulsively. It took her hours to clean the kitchen after each meal so to avoid the work, her cooking became simple and uninteresting. Although he resented spending the money, Alan began to bring home take-out food to prevent her from hav-ing to wash and clean the kitchen for hours after cooking. Every evening, Alan would sit by himself, reading the newspaper or watching television; then he would go to bed and continue watch-ing television by himself, eventually falling asleep alone while Joan was still busy cleaning.

Exasperated with Joan's behavior, he asked her to go to ther-apy and paid for two years of unsuccessful treatment. When they consulted me, I suggested the following procedure. Joan would clean carefully every day from nine to five, like any normal work day. At five she would shower and dress, so she would look nice when her husband came home. Then they would go out to dinner. If she did any cleaning after five o'clock, she would cook dinner at home and immediately go to bed with her husband. Alan objected that going out to dinner every night was too expensive. I said that they could pay for the dinners with the money they saved because Joan would no longer be in therapy. I also suggested that for every three months that Joan didn't clean after five o'clock, Alan would invite her to a brief vacation.

Alan said that he now realized that perhaps the cleaning had something to do with him, and he had to make some changes. They left my office cheerfully and called me some time later to tell me that cleaning was no longer a problem.

Alan preferred to pay for dinners rather than endless therapy. Joan preferred to go out rather than clean. By linking Joan's compulsive cleaning to Alan's stinginess, I managed to negotiate change.

Adolescents and Young Adults

As children become adolescents, their increasing responsibilities are rewarded with a share of the family belongings. The adolescent may begin to insist on receiving an increasingly higher allowance, using the family car, or sleeping over without asking permission. Also, the young person may want to have a say in the family's decision making, influencing, for example, how much the family will spend on a vacation.

As young people begin to have power, they sometimes discover that there are injustices in the family. Siblings may be treated differently or unfairly. There may be injustice between the parents. Often the unfairness relates to money. Typically, a young person will want to negotiate these injustices with the family, so everyone is treated the same. Parents, on the other hand, may see the young person's efforts as violations of the family hierarchy and refuse to discuss issues of injustice. At this point, some young people decide to leave home and get away from the family conflicts. Others decide to stay to fight for justice. And as they fail to negotiate with their parents, they may turn to irrational behaviors as a bold protest for change.

As with the couples just described, a young person's protests may involve active or passive behaviors. Typical active protests are stealing money, drug abuse, and other forms of delinquency. Passive resistance usually takes the form of failure at school or physical and emotional illness.

Delinquency

Martine was the middle child in a family with three children. Her older brother, John, and her younger sister, Kim, were attractive, popular, and successful at school. Martine, however, was fat and had a learning disability. She worried about her parents who were also overweight and had health problems. The parents always turned to Martine for everything they needed. By the time she was sixteen, she was cleaning, cooking, and doing the laundry for the family, besides going to school and holding a part-time job. Curiously, the parents didn't expect John or Kim to work or do chores.

Perhaps Martine had grown fat and developed a learning problem because the parents expected her to be the one that would stay home to take care of them, instead of having dates and going off to college. Perhaps the opposite was true, and the parents expected Martine to stay home and take care of them, because she could not date and wasn't smart enough to pursue higher education. Whatever the cause, Martine was treated differently from her siblings and carried an unfair burden.

Martine suffered because of her situation, yet it was difficult for her to verbalize her problems or negotiate with her parents. She just complained that she was unhappy with herself. She worked at a cash register of a department store and brought home the money she made to contribute to the family finances. One day it was discovered that she had been regularly stealing money from the cash register for a total of $2,000.

The store pressed charges, and the parents had to make restitution. Martine couldn't explain what she had done with the money. The mother was furious because she had to give up an expensive diet program in order to return the money to the store. The family was ordered to therapy.

The therapist realized that by stealing, Martine was making the parents pay for their injustice. Unable to negotiate her position in the family, Martine had behaved irrationally. The therapist influenced the parents, brother, and sister to understand that they had been unfair. They apologized to Martine and made a contract by which all three children shared the family chores equally. When Martine felt the family was fair to her, she stopped behaving irrationally.

Gambling

Jack was the black sheep of the family. Because his high school grades weren't good, his father said he would have to pay his own way to college. Instead, Jack began to borrow money from his mother and aunt allegedly to pay for school. But the family soon discovered that he was gambling away the money at the horse races.

When his mother and aunt refused to give him any more money, he borrowed from friends. Soon the friends were asking for the money back, and Jack told his family tearfully that these friends were really thugs who were threatening his life. He had to pay or else. Jack's bad habits were now costing the father much more than what it would have cost him to put Jack through school, as he had done for his other children.

The family consulted me, uncertain about whether to give Jack the money to pay his debts and worried about what they now realized was a serious gambling habit. I realized that two problems were apparent in the family. One was the issue of the father's injustice toward Jack. The other was the issue of Jack's gambling.

I decided to focus on the gambling first. I asked the father to give Jack the money to pay his debts with the condition that the young man would have to follow my instructions with respect to gambling. Every Sunday, his mother and aunt would go with him to the races and pick the horse that he would bet on. They would make their choice based on the attractiveness of the horse, or the jockey, or simply their intuition. As they observed the horses, they would instruct Jack loudly, so all his gambling buddies would know that the two old ladies were telling him what to do.

My thinking was that Jack would be so embarrassed in front of his gambling friends that he would develop an aversion to the horse races. I knew that simply telling a gambler to stop gambling doesn't work. But with the intrusion of the mother and the aunt, the whole context of gambling would be different and unpleasant.

As these plans were implemented, Jack became disgusted with gambling. He became interested in going back to school, and I helped him to negotiate with the father how this time, he would pay for Jack's education.

Taking Bribes

Ginnie resented her parents because they never gave her anything. They never had to. Ginnie's grandfather was very old and quite well off. He had decided to give away his money during his lifetime to his two grandchildren. So Ginnie's education, car, rent, and other expenses were paid by her grandfather. Ginnie thought it was unfair that her parents didn't have to sacrifice to put her through college, as she knew the parents of her friends were doing. She felt unloved by her parents and began to behave self-destructively.

After a series of difficult relationships with men who treated her badly, she began to obsess about her weight. She dieted to the point of starvation, and then she binged and made herself vomit. Over several years, the parents paid large amounts of money for her therapy and medical bills.

Finally, one therapist met with the parents and asked them to do the following. Every week they would get a report from Ginnie as to whether she had vomited. If not, each parent would give her a check for $250. So Ginnie would be making $500 a week simply by not vomiting. The parents did as they were asked, and Ginnie stopped vomiting. She was making her parents pay by receiving money instead of making them pay by hurting herself. Yet as soon as Ginnie seemed to be OK and the parents stopped paying her, she started vomiting again. The parents decided to continue paying her for two years after she had stopped vomiting, and they finally succeeded in breaking her habit.

How to Deal with Irrational Behavior

Politicians constantly rely on polls to check their power and effectiveness. As time goes by, the politician constantly draws on the support of followers to negotiate with the opposition.

In contrast, the dictator uses followers' support to avoid negotiating with the opposition. Because the dictator doesn't negotiate, he or she provokes irrational behavior in opponents. The consequence is that the opposition expresses itself through violence, which in turn leads to a violent response by the dictator.

Family leaders (spouses, parents, or elders) need to think like politicians, not dictators. They must constantly take the pulse of their family members to verify that they are sensitive to current needs. They must negotiate with those who might be turning from followers into opponents. If this doesn't happen, the family leader becomes a dictator who provokes irrational behavior of those in opposition and the violence that inevitably follows.

When irrational behavior has already occurred, the family leader needs to behave like a skillful politician rather than a dictator. You can prevent irrational behavior in your family or correct it if it's already happening by taking the following steps.

Step 1: Take Polls

Talk with your spouse and children together and separately. Find out about their financial needs, opinions, and changes in their thinking. Listen carefully, and make sure you understand them without making any judgments. Find out whether they are happy in their relationship with you or with each other.

Most importantly, find out whether an injustice has occurred in the family or whether anyone feels that there has been an injustice. Unfairness is the single biggest source of irrational behavior.

Step 2: Detect Irrational Behavior

If someone in the family is engaging in behavior that is destructive or doesn't make sense; when you ask them to stop, and they can't; or when you ask them why they do it, and they don't have an answer—that's irrational behavior. When people steal, gamble compulsively, binge and vomit, clean frenetically, don't clean at all, suffer from imaginary illnesses, and can't stop, they are behaving irrationally. Irrational behavior is a sign that something is wrong in the family relationships. It means that someone feels powerless, and therefore someone must be too powerful.

Step 3: Review Previous Negotiations

In order to discover a clue to the cause of the irrational behavior of a family member, review the last ten negotiations that took place in the family and assess their outcome. Specifically, look into negotiations about money. If the same person won all or most of the negotiations, or refused to listen and negotiate, or refused to modify their own position, that family member has too much power. If one person lost all negotiations, or wasn't heard, or didn't have needs met, that family member has too little power. One can expect that the person who presents irrational behavior is the one who feels powerless or destitute. You will also find out in relation to whom the person is powerless. This tells you which relationship must change and whom you must empower.

What to Say About $

Step 4: Change Yourself

You might discover that you, yourself, are the cause of the irrational behavior of a family member and that you are the one who has to change. You might have failed to give, listen, understand, accept the other's point of view, and negotiate. You need to renegotiate all those issues about which other family members believe that you were insensitive or unfair.

Step 5: Determine When Others Must Change

Your son may behave irrationally in relation to a conflict with his mother. Your daughter might be upset with her brother. You need to discover what has to be renegotiated and you have to arrange a renegotiation. Both parties will have to compromise, and you need to be the intermediary so they can negotiate.

Chapter Twelve

Epilogue

This book has shown how money plays an important and often covert role in determining our relationships. It can bring us close or alienate us from those we love, since everything we do with money has consequences for others.

We have tried to reveal the hidden meaning of money—the meaning that isn't apparent in our everyday transactions but has to do with emotions, passions, secret desires, guilt, and particularly love.

In many lives money is the main currency of love. When we love, we try to get something and also to give something. This double aim is what makes love complicated. Similarly, money influences our lives in ways that can make us either selfish or altruistic. But whereas in relationships we can love and also be loved, with money we often have to choose between selfishness and altruism.

Each of us leads a private life in relation to money, a hidden life for which there may be no external evidence. Inside each of us there may be a secret miser or philanthropist. We may be tortured by excruciating guilt or tormented by desire. Happiness and misery are part of the hidden meaning of money. Everyone has a personal relationship with money, and for many of us this relationship determines the nature of all our other relationships. We have thought about the secret meaning of money as involving a set of dimensions that go from one extreme to another. For example, money can be used to express hostility or love, to help, or to exploit. Whatever we choose to express through money determines the nature of our relationships.

Yet in human relations, nothing is ever all black or white—where there is love, there is hate—and power is always associated with dependence. As soon as one appears to have expressed a position without ambiguities, the opposite interpretation comes to mind and appears equally feasible. It may be that to have money *and* loving relationships, we need to be particularly tolerant of ambiguities.

In concluding this book, we would like to present a brief review of a few fundamental rules we believe a person must understand and accept in order to use money wisely in the family.

Rule 1: Money conflicts are often not really about money. If you have a conflict about money in your family, look beneath the surface. Are you trying to control your spouse or your children? Are they trying to control you? Has there been an injustice? Is someone trying to buy love? People sometimes quarrel about money to avoid arguing about more painful issues. You can only solve a financial conflict when you have discovered what it's truly about.

Rule 2: Family conflicts about various issues are often really about money. If you are having conflicts in your family, the root cause may be money. Marital unhappiness and problems with children may appear to be about love, dependence, or communication, but the real conflict may be about money.

Rule 3: Money can be both a deterrent and a reward. Don't hesitate to use it, when appropriate, to solve problems. The possibility of monetary gain or financial loss is strong motivation to change.

Rule 4: There is no perfect way to handle money. Because money has so many secret meanings, it represents different things to different people, and the meanings change with time. It's impossible to totally avoid misunderstandings and conflicts about money in the family.

Rule 5: Money can make you miserable. People who confuse money with love pay a high price. Don't demand money when you want love, and don't give money when you need to give love.

Rule 6: Growing up means giving. We all have to make the transition from the receiving end to the giving end of relationships. If you don't make this transition, you will have trouble with your spouse and children. Trust your strength and power enough to allow your generosity to emerge.

Rule 7: Giving means creating needs. Be careful about which needs you create in your children.

Rule 8: Giving to take away produces resentment and anger. When you give to your children and later punish them by taking away what you gave, you can produce resentments that can last a lifetime and may ensure your children's failure.

Rule 9: Flexibility leads to better relationships. Rigid "supposed to's" about money choke relationships. Accept that people have different expectations about money and you'll be happier.

Rule 10: Trying to reform your spouse is usually futile. A miser will be a miser, a spender will be a spender, and they will probably be married to each other. Your spouse behaves in a certain way because you behave in a complementary way. If you want to change the other, you have to start by changing yourself.

Rule 11: Mistrust scares people away. Those who bring to the second marriage the suspicion and mistrust they developed in the first marriage will turn off the second spouse.

Rule 12: Money cannot give you self-esteem. It's how you use money in relation to others that can make you hate or love yourself.

Rule 13: Using money for fun is OK. People who have happy marriages enjoy spending money together within the context of their own particular situation. The same applies to using money to have fun with your children. But enjoying money takes initiative. Learn to enjoy what you have without undue fear of loss.

Rule 14: People love those who love people more than money. If you want happiness, let people always be more important to you than money.

Rule 15: People who really listen are irresistible. Look for secret meanings and hidden conflicts. When you let your family members unburden themselves without harsh judgment, you may discover and resolve all kinds of tensions and resentments about money.

To make smart decisions about money in relationships, you need to have the courage to challenge the hidden beliefs and expectations that may have served to narrow your vision and opportunities for many years. We have found these rules, when implemented, have a liberating effect and can enable you to use money in ways that are conducive to fulfilling relationships.

Notes

Chapter One. Introduction: The Challenge of Money

1. Donald Trump describes his vocation in Donald Trump and Tony Schwartz, *Trump:The Art of the Deal* (New York: Random House, 1987).
2. For an interesting discussion of money and spirituality, see Jacob Needleman, *Money and the Meaning of Life* (New York: Doubleday, 1991).
3. A fascinating discussion of created wants can be found in John Kenneth Galbraith, *The Affluent Society* (New York: New American Library, 1984).
4. An interesting fictional treatment of created wants can be found in Stephen King (*Needful Things*, NAL/Dutton 1992).

Chapter Two. Money and the Young Couple

1. For more on solving marital problems, see Chapter Three, "Marital Problems: Balancing Power," in my book *Strategic Family Therapy* (San Francisco: Jossey-Bass, 1981).

Chapter Three. Money and Our Difficult Parents

1. A method for working with sex offenders and their victims is described in my book *Sex, Love and Violence* (New York: Norton, 1990).

Chapter Five. Money and the Middle Years

1. For an interesting discussion of the fear of financial loss see Barbara Ehrenreich, *Fear of Falling: The Inner Life of the Middle Class* (New York: Pantheon Books, 1989).
   The fear of falling from social class was described as early as 1942 by Margaret Mead. See Margaret Mead, "And Keep Your Powder Dry!", in *The Member of the Upper Class* (New York: Morrow, 1942, 1965).
2. For more on negotiating in marriage, see James P. Keim, "Triangulation and the Art of Negotiation," in the *Journal of Systemic Therapies* (Ontario, Canada, Winter 1993).

Chapter Ten. The Positive Use of Money

1. For other unusual and humorous ways of solving relationship problems, see Chapter Four, "Finding the Humorous Alternative," and Chapter Five, "Choosing the Right Strategy," in my book *Behind the One-Way Mirror: Advances in the Practice of Strategic Therapy* (San Francisco: Jossey-Bass, 1984).

Index

The Authors

Cloé Madanes is one of the world's most respected authorities on marital and family relationships and on the process of change in families. She directs the Family Therapy Institute of Washington, D.C., located in Rockville, Maryland, and is a distinguished lecturer, consultant, and workshop leader. Her books, *Strategic Family Therapy*, *Behind the One-Way Mirror*, and *Sex, Love and Violence*, have won international acclaim and have been published in more than six languages.

Claudio Madanes is a movie director and stock market expert in Buenos Aires, Argentina.

The authors are sister and brother.

Communications to the authors or requests for information about their seminars should be addressed to the Family Therapy Institute, 5850 Hubbard Drive, Rockville, Maryland, 20852.